THE ILLUSTRATED HISTORY OF THE WORLD

The Middle Ages

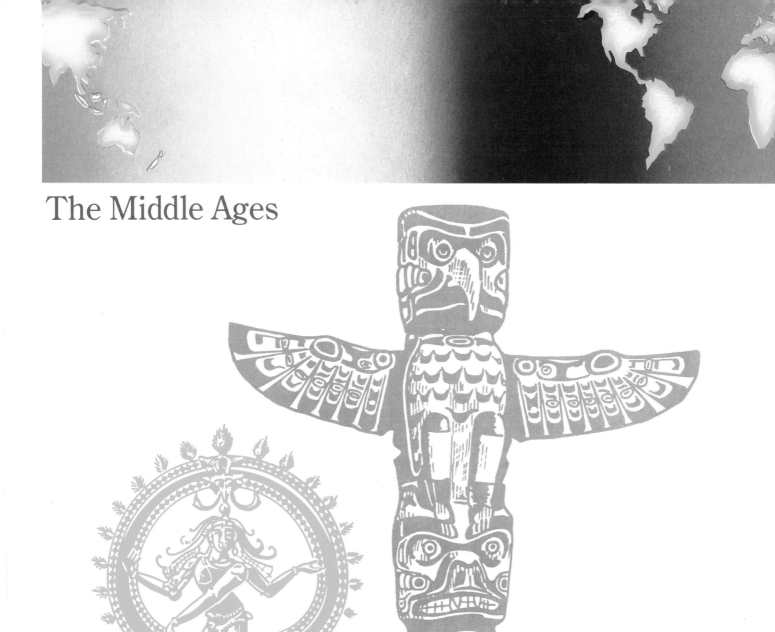

PREFACE

The Illustrated History of the World is a unique series of eight volumes covering the entire scope of human history, from the days of the nomadic hunters up to the present. Each volume surveys significant events and personages, key political and economic developments, and the critical forces that inspired change, in both institutions and the everyday life of people around the globe.

The books are organized on a spread-by-spread basis, allowing ease of access and depth of coverage on a wide range of fascinating topics and time periods within any one volume. Each spread serves as a kind of mini-essay, in words and pictures, of its subject. The text—cogent, concise and lively—is supplemented by an impressive array of illustrations (original art, full-color photographs, maps, diagrams) and features (glossary, index, time charts, further reading listings). Taking into account the new emphasis on multicultural education, special care has been given to presenting a balanced portrait of world history: the volumes in the series explore all civilizations—whether it's the Mayans in Mexico, the Shoguns in Japan or the Sumerians in the Middle East.

The Middle Ages

Fiona Macdonald

Facts On File

The Middle Ages

Macdonald, Fiona
The Middle Ages/Fiona Macdonald.
p. cm.
"The Illustrated history of the world"—Jacket.
Previously published: Hemel Hempstead Hertfordshire:
Simon & Shuster Young Books, 1991.
Includes bibliographical references and index.
Summary: Text and illustrations explore the history of the world from
the Mongol invasions through the voyages of Christopher Columbus.
ISBN 0-8160-2788-9
1. Middle Ages—History—Juvenile literature.
[1. Middle Ages—History.] I. Title.
II. Title: Illustrated history of the world.
D117.M2 1993
909.07—dc20
91-43094

You can find Facts On File on the World Wide Web at
http://www.factsonfile.com

Facts On File books are available at special discounts when purchased
in bulk quantities for businesses, associations, institutions or sales
promotions. Please call our Special Sales Department in New York at
212/967-8800 or 800/322-8755.

Designed by Hammond Hammond
Composition by Goodfellow and Egan Ltd. Cambridge
Printed and bound in Slovenia
by DELO – tiskarna d. d.
by arrangement with Korotan – Ljubljana

10 9 8 7 6 5 4 3 2

This book is printed on acid-free paper.

First Published in Great Britain in 1991 by
Simon and Schuster Young Books

CONTENTS

INTRODUCTION

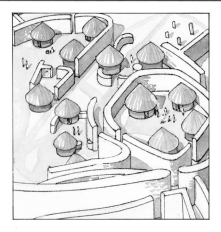

This book looks at the history of the world during the Middle Ages, that is, from around AD 1100 to AD 1500. It is divided into two sections. Part One concentrates on the first 200 years of the period, up to approximately AD 1300. Part Two examines the years between AD 1300–AD 1500, a period sometimes known as the Later Middle Ages.

During the Middle Ages, brilliant literary cultures–based on books, accounts and other written records–developed in western Europe, the Muslim lands of the Middle East, and in China. We can find out a lot about life in these countries from the numerous documents that survive, as well as from buildings, paintings and *physical remains*.

In other parts of the world–North and South America, much of Africa, and Southeast Asia–written records are more sparse, but this does not mean that 'civilizations' there were any less developed. *Archaeological* evidence tells us that new lands were brought under cultivation, great cities and empires flourished, and many beautiful objects–often with a religious purpose–were made by skilled craftsmen and women.

We have no written evidence to tell us about the remaining areas of the world–Australia and some of the neighboring islands, the southern desert lands of Africa, and the far, frozen north of Asia. In comparison with other countries, these areas were scantily populated. The people who lived there followed what might appear to be a rather simple way of life.

But in recent years, *archaeologists* and *anthropologists* have discovered that these peoples' lifestyles were finely balanced and very well suited to the harsh environments surrounding them. They have also shown that these peoples had a rich and imaginative culture, based on traditional myths, legends, stories and dreams. They expressed themselves and their culture in songs, ceremonies, cave drawings, clothing, jewelry, masks, makeup and body-painting.

SCANDINAVIA

RUSSIA

EUROPE

ASIA

NORTH AFRICA

JAPAN

CHINA

ARABIA

INDIA

PART ONE

Three Great Civilizations

Part One of this book looks at three great civilizations which flourished between AD 1100–1350. In western Europe, society was organized according to a *feudal system*; everyone, from the greatest noble to the lowliest peasant, was allowed to occupy their land only in return for paying some sort of rent or performing some sort of service. Nobles owed their feudal service (leading troops in battle) directly to the king; peasants owed theirs (doing farm work) to the nobleman or woman who had been granted the local great estate by the king. The Church was the other great force in western European civilization. Clergymen were the best educated people in Europe. They played an important part in government, as well as offering spiritual guidance and advice.

ISLAM In the medieval Muslim world, which stretched from southern Spain to the borders of China, law, government, art, literature and learning were all shaped by the teachings of the Islamic faith. People from many different backgrounds were linked together by this shared culture and medieval Muslim achievements in mathematics, science and technology were admired and imitated around the world.

CHINA In the East, another brilliant and advanced civilization developed in Sung China, and influenced many of the neighboring lands. Chinese technological discoveries, such as printing, gunpowder and paper money, were far in advance of anything known in the western world.

Chinese silks, porcelain and spices were exported to Europe and the Muslim world, where they were highly prized. In this way, trade linked these three great medieval civilizations, and allowed their people, as well as their ideas and inventions, to make contact with one another.

POPULATION GROWTH AND PROSPERITY During the years 1100–1300, many countries in different parts of the world grew rich and prosperous. Populations increased, towns expanded, farming and trading became more profitable, and wealthy patrons paid for many beautiful buildings, paintings and other works of art.

The Western World
EUROPE: COUNTRIES AND PEOPLES

Norman knights, from the Bayeux 'Tapestry,' embroidered c.1100 by a group of noblewomen to record the Norman conquest of England in 1066. The tapestry shows the events leading up to the Norman invasion, and the decisive Battle of Hastings, in 'comic strip' form. It is over 75 yards long.

Under their leader, Duke William, Norman forces invaded and occupied England. The Norman language, customs, and ideas about government rapidly became mixed with local English traditions, and laid the foundations for the medieval civilization of England.

A NEW ERA But, by 1100, when this book begins, the centuries of pirate raids and large-scale invasions of Europe were almost over. In many European states, settled governments and freedom from outside attack led to a period of growth and expansion. Populations increased, new lands were cleared for farming, towns prospered, and trade and manufacturing industries became increasingly important. There was money to spare for building castles, churches, city walls and great cathedrals. Kings and government officials passed new laws and developed new ways to administer the countries they ruled.

The 12th and 13th centuries are often called the 'High Middle Ages' in Europe. This is because they were a time of peace, growth and stability, compared to the restless and often violent years that had just passed.

During the years 700–1050, the peoples of Europe had lived through civil wars and *dynastic* disputes in France and Germany. They had faced invasions by *nomadic Magyar* tribes from the east, and by *Muslim* forces, based in Arabia and North Africa, from the south and west. Most damaging of all, they had suffered repeated pirate raids and savage attacks from roving bands of warriors–the Vikings of Scandinavia.

THE VIKINGS The last major Viking raid in Europe was the Norman attack on England in 1066. The Normans were Vikings, who had settled in Northern France.

THE BATTLES GO ON Even so, war and the disruption it brought to the lives of ordinary people had not completely vanished from Europe. In England and France, kings struggled to win new territory, or, sometimes, simply to stay in power. In Spain, Italy and southern France, local armies fought to recapture lands conquered by Muslim rulers.

The great Byzantine Empire in eastern Europe was constantly on the alert against attack by its great trading rivals, the Italian city states of Venice and Genoa, or by Muslim forces from the Middle East.

And on the northeastern frontiers of Europe, the great Russian kingdom centered on the city of Kiev was repeatedly threatened by nomad invaders sweeping westward across the plains of central Asia.

Europe in 1100

SCANDINAVIA

BRITAIN

●LONDON

POLAND

ATLANTIC
OCEAN

FRANCE

●VENICE
●GENOA

ITALY

SPAIN

●CORDOBA

BLACK SEA

●CONSTANTINOPLE

TURKEY

MEDITERRANEAN SEA

KIEV ●

Modern Europe

NORWAY   SWEDEN

EIRE   GREAT   NETHERLANDS   USSR
       BRITAIN
BELGIUM   GERMANY   POLAND
                              CZECHOSLOVAKIA
FRANCE   HUNGARY
SWITZERLAND   AUSTRIA   ROMANIA
                    YUGOSLAVIA   BULGARIA
SPAIN   GREECE   TURKEY
PORTUGAL   SYRIA
                                 LEBANON
MOROCCO   ISRAEL   JORDAN
      ALGERIA   TUNISIA
              LIBYA   EGYPT

The countries of
Europe, c.1100 AD,
compared with a
modern map of
Europe. During the
Middle Ages, wars,
boundary disputes,
quarrels over
inheritance and
marriage alliances
all helped to shape
the boundaries of
European countries
as we know them
today.

Lands under Norman rule	Lands under Muslim rule
Holy Roman Empire	Lands under Seljuk rule
Byzantine Empire	

Left. The Byzantine
emperor John II
Comnenus, from a
mosaic picture in
the great church
(now a mosque) of
Santa Sophia in
Constantinople
(present-day
Istanbul, in Turkey).
He was a successful
ruler, who made
treaties with
neighboring
Muslim states to
protect the frontier
lands of his
empire, and so
preserved its
power.

Key Viking Dates

c. 600–700	Growth of powerful Viking kingdoms in Scandinavia
793	First Viking raid on England
841	Vikings settle in Dublin, Ireland
911	Viking leader Rollo gains large territory in Normandy, France
982	Viking emperors settle in Greenland
c. 1000	Viking sailors cross the Atlantic Ocean and reach Newfoundland in Canada
1014–1035	Viking King Cnut the Great rules over an empire in Norway, Sweden, Denmark and England
1090	Normans invade and conquer Sicily, important center of international trade
c.1100	Growth of separate, independent kingdoms of Norway, Sweden and Denmark. End of Viking raids

Above. Viking
longships were
designed and built to
carry passengers
and cargo, as well as
raiders across the
stormy northern
seas.

Left. Viking gravestone, from Gotland,
Sweden, showing scenes from Viking
mythology and a warship with a fully
armed crew.

A LIVING FROM THE LAND

Peasants harvesting barley on their lord's land. They are using sickles, with sharp, curved blades to cut the straw. The man with the big stick is the lord's *reeve*, or overseer. He is giving orders and organizing the harvest work.

What was life like for the people who lived in Europe during the High Middle Ages? Most people worked on the land, growing food and rearing livestock. It was hard, dirty and heavy work, but essential if enough food was to be produced to feed Europe's growing population.

Men, women and, sometimes, children labored in the fields, ploughing, sowing and harvesting corn; making hay to feed cattle and horses; gathering grapes to make wine; and picking apples and pears to provide welcome sweetness during the winter. Women made salty, pungent cheese from the milk provided by cows, sheep and goats. Fish were caught along the coast, and were preserved by salting, or hung outside to dry.

NEW TECHNOLOGY Power–to pull ploughs, carry loads, chop down trees or clear new lands–was provided by men and animals. There were few machines to help them, although some important inventions, such as windmills (for grinding corn) and water-powered fulling mills (used in making cloth), were developed at this time. Women kneaded bread, dug gardens, plucked chickens and skinned rabbits, churned milk, sheared sheep and spun wool, as well as looking after their homes, their husbands and their children.

HOUSES AND BUILDINGS Ordinary peoples' houses were made of strong, heavy timbers, sawn and shaped

A typical medieval village in northern Europe. The villagers' houses are grouped around the church. Each house had its own little garden, where vegetables were grown, and chickens and perhaps bees were kept. The largest house in the village belonged to the local lord. Unlike the villagers' homes, it had separate rooms for eating, sleeping and relaxing, and a proper chimney. Wealthy lords might have houses or castles in several villages. They travelled round from one house to another, leaving their staff of estate managers, farmhands and servants to manage everything while they were away. The villagers made their living by working in the fields surrounding the village. Land was often farmed in big 'open' fields, rather than in small, separate, enclosed plots. It was easier to plough and to gather in the harvest that way. Each villager had several strips, divided by ditches, fences or boundary stones. They worked together in the fields; that way, everyone stood a chance of growing a good crop.

Population Levels

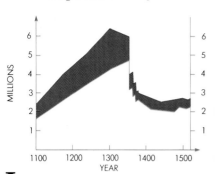

In comparison with the present-day, medieval population levels were very low. In AD 1000 the total population of Europe was around 38 or 39 million. (Today it is around 450 million.)

By the middle of the 14th century, the European population had almost doubled in size, to around 74 million. Plagues and famines then caused a dramatic fall, of perhaps 25 million, and the population did not regain its pre-plague size until the late 16th century.

The graph above details these changes for medieval England.

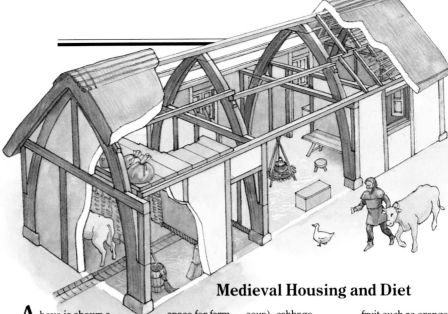

Medieval Housing and Diet

Above is shown a typical medieval village house. One end was used for eating and sleeping; the other was used as a barn, with stalls for cattle, and storage space for farm equipment and food.

The typical medieval diet in northern Europe consisted of bread, cheese, dried peas and beans (made into soup), cabbage, onions, garlic, apples, and pears, with watery ale to drink. Eggs, meat and fresh fish were luxuries.

In southern Europe, wine, soft fruit such as oranges, and olives provided welcome variety. When the harvest failed, or animals fell sick, people went hungry.

by hand, and fitted together with the help of friends and neighbors. The spaces between the timbers were filled with a sticky mass of clay, straw and horsehair, 'puddled' together by stirring and trampling underfoot. In places where timber was scarce, houses were made of rough stone, often with slate or turf for roofs.

SOCIAL STRUCTURE In many parts of Europe, ordinary people did not own their own plots of land. Instead, they occupied them as tenants of the local lord. They paid him rent (in money, produce, or by working a set number of days on his farm) for the right to live and work in 'their' houses and fields. Some people were tied to the land because they were owned by the lord, in the same way that he owned horses and cattle. These men and women could not marry, move house or travel without his permission, and, usually, without paying him a sizeable fee for the privilege.

THE RELIGIOUS WORLD

During the Middle Ages, Christian missionaries finally reached the far corners of Europe, and completed a process of *conversion* that had been going on for hundreds of years. It is hard to find out exactly what ordinary people believed. Probably many more people then than nowadays went to church regularly and said their prayers. They also gave money to build and decorate their local churches, and to support their local priests and religious charities.

But sometimes their Christian beliefs were mixed with the remains of old, *pagan* superstitions, and their understanding of the Church's religious teachings was rather confused.

THE ROLE OF THE CHURCH The Church was the most powerful institution in medieval Europe. Unlike kings and princes, it did not die, and could not easily be overthrown. Instead, it lasted from generation to generation. The head of the western Church was the Pope, who was Bishop of Rome. (Christians in eastern Europe obeyed a different leader, based in Constantinople–present-day Istanbul.)

The Pope ruled over a group of powerful Church officials in all the countries of Europe. There were frequent quarrels between the Pope and local rulers, when they disagreed over political issues, or on matters of Church business. In England, King Henry I gave orders for the English Archbishop Thomas Becket to be murdered, because Becket sided with the Pope and disobeyed the king.

THE WEALTH OF THE CHURCH The Church was also the biggest landowner in Europe. Wealthy, pious men and women gave land, houses, farms and vineyards to the

Above. Pope Urban II (1042–99) consecrates (blesses and pronounces sacred) the new church buildings at the great monastery of Cluny, in Burgundy, now part of France. You can see him on the left of the picture, wearing a golden robe. Cluny was rich, powerful and very influential in medieval Europe.

One of its greatest abbots, St Benedict, introduced a new set of rules teaching monks and nuns how to live. These were widely copied and set a standard that lasted for many centuries.

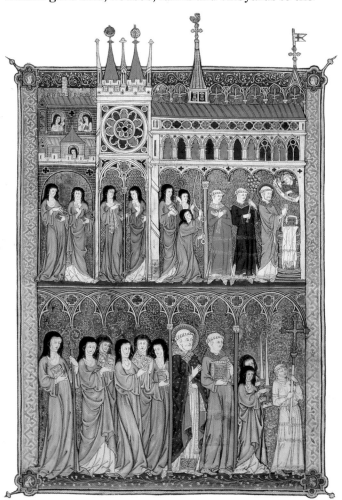

Right. Nuns and priests walking in procession on their way to a church service. One nun is busy ringing the bells to summon everyone to prayer; you can see her pulling on the bell-ropes in the center of the picture. The sacristan (responsible for all the holy objects in the nuns' church) carries her keys.

Church. They hoped that God would reward their generosity with a place in heaven. They also won fame and admiration among their fellow Christians while they were still alive. Kings, queens and wealthy nobles competed with one another to build the most beautiful chapel, or the most noble church tower. They gave many rich and precious gifts to their local churches and cathedrals, and, in some cases, contributed large sums of money to pay for architects and craftsmen to design a whole new building in the latest, most fashionable style.

CHRISTIAN ART Many religious treasures have survived from the Middle Ages: gold and silver crosses, brilliant stained and painted glass, fine carvings and statues, *relics* of saints encased in jewel-studded boxes, sumptuous embroideries, and wonderfully decorated manuscripts containing Bible stories, hymns and prayers. These were produced by craftsmen in the towns, and also by monks and nuns, working in religious communities shut away from the world.

POPE

CARDINALS/ARCHBISHOPS

BISHOPS

PRIESTS   ABBOTS/ABBESSES   FRIARS

DEACONS AND MINOR ORDERS   MONKS   NUNS

Hierarchy of the Medieval Church

The medieval church was a strict *hierarchy*. There were several different grades of clergy, with great differences of wealth and power among them. All clergymen began their career in the church as deacons and then became priests. A few progressed further to become bishops or archbishops, and a tiny minority might also be appointed cardinal and, eventually, Pope.

Left. Cathedrals are among the most beautiful and impressive buildings to survive from the medieval period. Architects experimented with daring and dramatic new structures, and invented ingenious new techniques to build, taller, lighter, more elegant designs.
A cathedral could take hundreds of years to build. Craftsmen working there had no power tools to help them. Stones and woodwork had to be laboriously cut and shaped by hand. Roofs and spires were covered in tiles, or coated with heavy lead sheeting.
Inside, great care and attention was paid to cathedral decoration. Walls were painted with scenes from the Bible. Brilliant stained glass was installed, and elaborately decorated tiles covered the floors. Men and women embroidered robes and hangings in silk and gold thread, and gold and jewels were used to make crosses to stand on the altar.

GOVERNMENT, LAW AND LEARNING

The Church acted as an important center of learning during the Middle Ages. Priests, monks and nuns studied and translated religious and philosophical texts; wrote books on religious topics; ran boarding schools for the children of wealthy parents; and acted as advisors to powerful men and women.

RELIGION AND EDUCATION Outside the enclosed world of monasteries and nunneries, students and teachers in all the great universities of Europe were enrolled in 'holy orders.' This meant that they had taken the first steps towards becoming a priest.

In fact, few of them took their religious careers any further. They went on, instead, to work as clerks, *scribes* and administrators for governments throughout Europe. Others became full-time scholars, seeking teaching jobs in schools and colleges, or worked as secretaries and private tutors in noble households.

THE CHANGE IN GOVERNMENT Kings and governments in Europe were becoming increasingly professional during the Middle Ages. In the past, rulers had relied on their loyal military commanders and on their household servants to carry out their orders. Now, educated men helped kings, nobles and local lords draft laws, keep accounts, collect taxes, compose important letters, conduct delicate negotiations, and discuss treaties and alliances between friendly nations. Kings also began to summon meetings of noblemen and representatives from the towns and the countryside to help them share the responsibility for decision-making, and to take the blame for unpopular measures such as higher taxes or harsh new laws.

THE ROLE OF KINGS Even with all these trained helpers, the personality and intelligence of each king was still tremendously important. He had to be able to understand national and international politics; to cope with the details of day-to-day administration; to know how to give orders that people would obey; and how to choose wise and prudent advisors. Most important of all, he had to win the trust, loyalty and affection of all his subjects. Often, the only way this could be done was by gifts and rewards.

Although the Church taught that kings were appointed by God, and that it was everyone's duty to obey them, a weak or foolish king found it difficult to gain support at home or allies abroad, and lived in constant fear of being overthrown.

King Edward I of England (1239–1307) at a meeting of Parliament. The king is surrounded by his nobles (in scarlet robes) and by the bishops (wearing pointed hats, called miters).

The First Universities in Europe

Key:
- Founded in the 1100s
- Founded in the 1200s
- Founded in the 1300s
- Founded in the 1400s

Map labels: NORTH SEA, UPPSALA, ST ANDREWS, SWEDEN, BALTIC SEA, DENMARK, BRITAIN, OXFORD, LOUVRAIN, GERMANY, POLAND, PARIS, ERFURT, PRAGUE, CRACOW, BASEL, VIENNA, FRANCE, PORTUGAL, VALLADOLID, MONTPELLIER, REGGIO, PECS, BOLOGNA, HUNGARY, HUNGARY, LISBON, SPAIN, ITALY, MEDITERRANEAN SEA, SALERNO, NORTH AFRICA, GREECE

Medieval Education

Universities were founded throughout Europe in the Middle Ages. The earliest universities were in southern Europe, but by the end of the medieval period they had been established in northern European countries as well. Paris (France) and Bologna (Italy) were probably the most famous and respected universities; students flocked to study there from many lands.

By present-day standards, medieval universities taught a narrow range of topics: theology, law, medicine, music and philosophy. Students prepared for their degrees by studying two groups of subjects: the *trivium* (which included linguistics, grammar and philosophy); and the *quadrivium*, which included mathematics, music and astronomy. Law and medicine were specialized extras. Most young people in medieval Europe did not go to school, let alone college. Parents taught poor children the practical skills they would need to earn a living; most medieval country people could not read or write, but these skills were sometimes learned by shopkeepers and other tradesmen living in towns.

Fourteenth-century carving from Italy, showing university students and their professor in a classroom. Italian universities were famous for their scholarship in medicine and law.

The Structure of Medieval Society

The most powerful person in any medieval society was the king or prince (or, very rarely a queen) who ruled the country.

Kings and princes relied on nobles to help them. They acted as war-leaders, governors of distant regions, and as senior government advisors. They were rewarded by kings with grants of land titles and other honors.

Knights were less wealthy and less powerful than the nobles, but played an important role, originally in war and later in local administration.

There was a small, but growing, professional group within medieval society – chiefly composed of lawyers and government administrators.

In towns, merchants and shopkeepers prospered.

But most men and women living in medieval Europe were poor, by modern standards. They occupied their land in return for money rent paid to the local landowner (a knight or noble), or in return for working on the landowner's farm. They also paid taxes – to the Church, to the king, and sometimes to the local lord. Some of these peasants were free; others were serfs. They 'belonged' to their lord, and could do little without his permission.

People without home, land or families to support them were at the bottom of medieval society. Beggars were a common sight, especially in towns.

5–10% KINGS, PRINCES, NOBLES, BISHOPS, ETC.
90–95% THE REST
5% THE VERY POOR

Structure of society in 1100

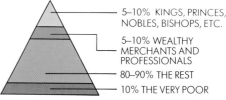

5–10% KINGS, PRINCES, NOBLES, BISHOPS, ETC.
5–10% WEALTHY MERCHANTS AND PROFESSIONALS
80–90% THE REST
10% THE VERY POOR

Structure of society in 1450

CHIVALRY: LOVE AND WAR

A Knight's Armor

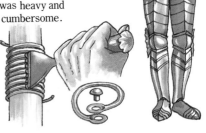

Medieval knights rode into battle wearing armor to protect themselves from attack by swords and spears.

Chain mail was made from interlocking wire rings (see below) worn over a thick leather jerkin. Later, armor was made of solid metal plates joined together. It encased the wearer completely, but it was heavy and cumbersome.

Left. The German nobleman, Heinrich von Anhalt (1170–1252) fighting with his companions at a tournament. Noble ladies look on while he prepares to 'unhorse' his opponent.

In medieval Europe, power was based on land ownership, and on the fighting men who could conquer and defend it. Medieval kings rewarded their faithful warriors, advisors and companions with gifts of land, as well as with titles and special privileges. These noblemen granted out smaller portions of their estates to their own followers, in return for a promise to fight alongside them when required.

In this way, men in the upper ranks of society became linked by ties of property and loyalty. The king could rely on his nobles to support him, otherwise he would take away their land. In turn, the nobles could rely (for the same reason) on a band of well armed followers, called *knights*, to accompany them in battle and assist them in local peacekeeping and *garrison* duties.

CHANGES IN THE MILITARY SYSTEM At first, the knights provided their own small private armies of ordinary soldiers. Foot soldiers, armed with bows and arrows, were also recruited from among poor farm laborers, workers in towns, outlaws, petty criminals and even prisoners. But by 1300, rulers throughout Europe had begun to hire professional soldiers, who would fight for anyone who paid them. Some knights preferred to pay a sum of money, rather than provide troops or ride to war. This, along with tolls and taxes, helped to pay for

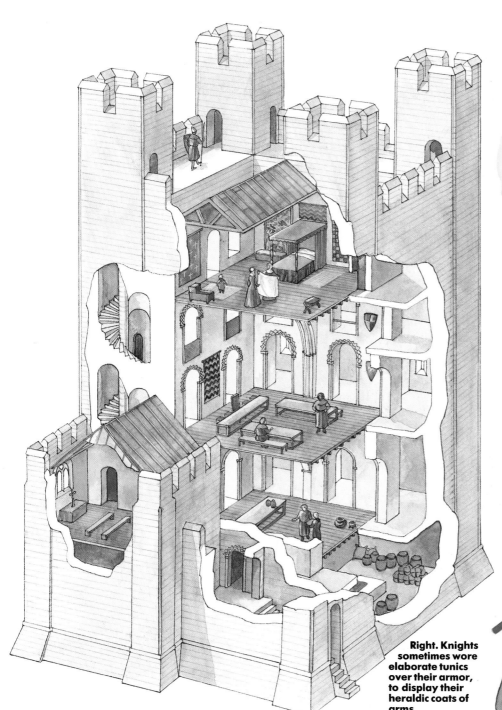

Castles were first built as military strongholds, and they continued to be important wartime fortresses throughout the Middle Ages. But, by the 14th century, they were beginning to develop into impressive family homes and centers of estate administration.

A large castle was like a town in miniature. It was surrounded by fields where food for the inhabitants was grown. Within the 'curtain' of its strong walls, there were: exercise yards for the castle garrison; a well to provide fresh water; a kitchen and bakery; various workshops; a blacksmith's forge; servants' housing; stables and barns; and perhaps even a pleasure garden where the castle ladies could stroll.

Right. Knights sometimes wore elaborate tunics over their armor, to display their heraldic coats of arms.

the costs of feeding and transporting the troops, and providing them with weapons.

THE IDEAL KNIGHT Even if some knights did not fight, the ties of loyalty between kings, great nobles and their knights were still very important. A code of behavior grew up, embodying all the characteristics of the ideal knight. He should be bold and brave, yet gentle, considerate, wise and courteous. He should be a ruthless fighter, but also fond of music, poetry and polite society. Preferably, he should be inspired by the love of some beautiful lady, whom he worshiped from afar. He should be a good Christian, and follow the teachings of the Church. His manners should be perfect, his speech smooth and entertaining, his appearance manly, strong, energetic and elegant.

Understandably, this ideal knight did not really exist. But he is a familiar figure in many medieval songs and stories, and tells us a lot about the qualities that people valued at the time.

Chivalry, as this code of behavior was called, applied to the upper classes only. Ordinary, rough soldiers were simply expected to shoot straight and obey orders.

EUROPE AT THE FRONTIERS

Christian armies loading troops and equipment onto a transport ship at a Mediterranean port, before sailing off to the Crusades. From a 14th century French manuscript.

We have seen that the 11th–13th centuries were a time of growth and stability within Europe. Even so, many European kings had to face opposition from powerful nobles within their kingdoms, or disputes with neighboring countries over the possession of land. For example, Germany was shaken by civil wars during the period 1070–1120, and England and France quarrelled frequently over the ownership of lands in Aquitaine, a region in southern France.

FRONTIER BATTLES   The situation was different for states on the frontiers of Europe. They were exposed to influences, and sometimes attacks, from non-European powers, whose languages, culture and faith were often completely different from their own.

SPAIN   These frontier contacts sometimes resulted in a rich new civilization. In southern Spain, which was governed by Muslim rulers for most of the Middle Ages, a well educated, multi-cultural and tolerant community developed.

Jews, Christians and Muslims lived peacefully side by side, and learned much from each others' traditions, skills and achievements.

But, inspired by their faith and by feelings of national pride, the Christian kings of northern Spain felt compelled to launch a series of attacks on the southern Muslim state which they felt was 'occupying' land that was rightfully theirs.

NORTHERN EUROPE   On the northern frontiers of Europe, conquests disturbed local cultures. German forces advanced northward and eastward into lands occupied by the Slav peoples, in present-day Poland and Lithuania. German settlements were also established to the southeast, in Czechoslovakia, and German emperors tried to increase their power and influence in Italy.

THE CRUSADES   Kings, knights and churchmen from all over Europe were involved in another series of invasions–the Crusades. During these wars, Christian troops attempted to capture the 'Holy Land,' as they called the territory surrounding the city of Jerusalem (in present-day Israel and Jordan), from the Muslim rulers.

The Crusades provide us with a good example of the typical medieval combination of high ideals, greed and brutal conduct. Undoubtedly, many soldiers joined the crusading armies because they wanted to see a Christian king ruling the land where Jesus had lived and died. But others hoped for the chance to win fame or rich plunder, or simply had a taste for adventure. The Christian troops disgraced themselves on several occasions by cruelty toward their Muslim enemies, and finally returned to Europe, defeated, in 1291.

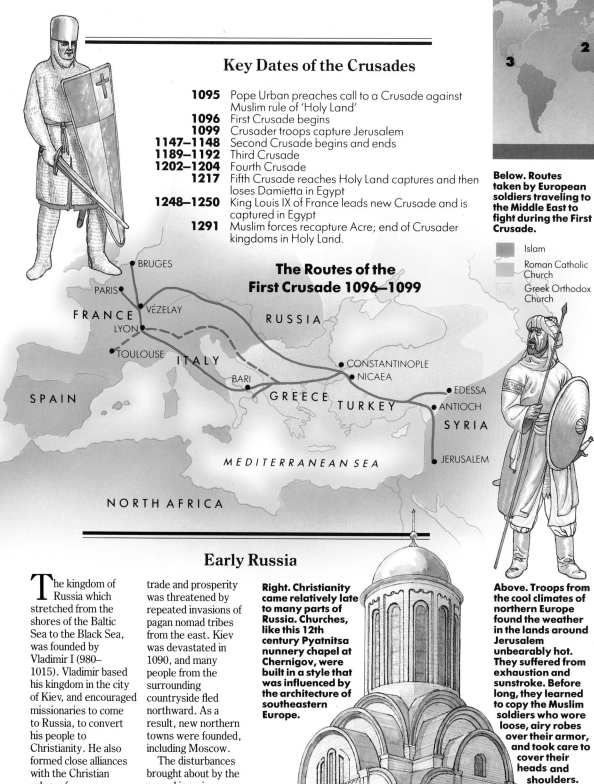

Key Dates of the Crusades

1095	Pope Urban preaches call to a Crusade against Muslim rule of 'Holy Land'
1096	First Crusade begins
1099	Crusader troops capture Jerusalem
1147–1148	Second Crusade begins and ends
1189–1192	Third Crusade
1202–1204	Fourth Crusade
1217	Fifth Crusade reaches Holy Land captures and then loses Damietta in Egypt
1248–1250	King Louis IX of France leads new Crusade and is captured in Egypt
1291	Muslim forces recapture Acre; end of Crusader kingdoms in Holy Land.

The Routes of the First Crusade 1096–1099

BRUGES
PARIS
VÉZELAY
FRANCE
LYON
TOULOUSE
ITALY
BARI
SPAIN
GREECE
RUSSIA
CONSTANTINOPLE
NICAEA
TURKEY
EDESSA
ANTIOCH
SYRIA
JERUSALEM
MEDITERRANEAN SEA
NORTH AFRICA

Below. Routes taken by European soldiers traveling to the Middle East to fight during the First Crusade.

Islam

Roman Catholic Church

Greek Orthodox Church

1 Around 1000, a great settlement in southern Africa began to emerge, called Great Zimbabwe. The settlement was founded on trade, and remains of luxury goods from as far away as China have been found in the excavations.

2 The Muslim Almoravid Dynasty expanded its power and influence in north Africa and southern Spain at the end of the 11th century. Troops were sent across the Sahara Desert to conquer the rich West African kingdom of Ghana.

3 During the twelfth century, the Toltec civilization flourished in Central America. The Toltec capital city of Tula was founded in present-day Mexico.

4 Around 1126 the prosperous and very advanced civilization of Sung China came to be threatened by the invading Chin peoples from the north. The Chin people occupied about one-third of Sung territory, including the capital, Kaifeng. The Sung were therefore forced to create a new capital at Hangchow.

Above. Troops from the cool climates of northern Europe found the weather in the lands around Jerusalem unbearably hot. They suffered from exhaustion and sunstroke. Before long, they learned to copy the Muslim soldiers who wore loose, airy robes over their armor, and took care to cover their heads and shoulders.

Early Russia

The kingdom of Russia which stretched from the shores of the Baltic Sea to the Black Sea, was founded by Vladimir I (980–1015). Vladimir based his kingdom in the city of Kiev, and encouraged missionaries to come to Russia, to convert his people to Christianity. He also formed close alliances with the Christian rulers of Constantinople.

Vladimir's son, King Yaroslav I (1019–54), encouraged trade and during his reign merchant cities such as Kiev, Novgorod and Lagoda grew rich. But in the years that followed, Russian

trade and prosperity was threatened by repeated invasions of pagan nomad tribes from the east. Kiev was devastated in 1090, and many people from the surrounding countryside fled northward. As a result, new northern towns were founded, including Moscow.

The disturbances brought about by the nomad invasions weakened the kingdom, and led to the emergence of several smaller states. The kingdom finally collapsed in 1240, when the city of Kiev was again destroyed, this time by Mongol invaders from central Asia.

Right. Christianity came relatively late to many parts of Russia. Churches, like this 12th century Pyatnitsa nunnery chapel at Chernigov, were built in a style that was influenced by the architecture of southeastern Europe.

The Islamic World
MANY PEOPLES, ONE FAITH

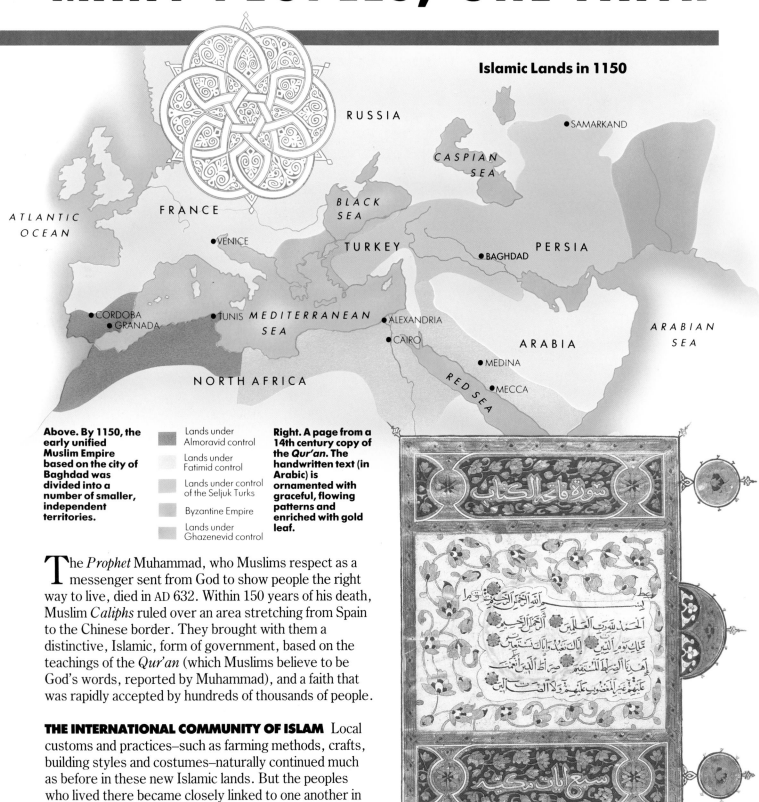

Islamic Lands in 1150

RUSSIA

SAMARKAND

CASPIAN SEA

BLACK SEA

FRANCE

ATLANTIC OCEAN

VENICE

TURKEY

PERSIA

BAGHDAD

CORDOBA
GRANADA

TUNIS

MEDITERRANEAN SEA

ALEXANDRIA

CAIRO

ARABIA

ARABIAN SEA

MEDINA

NORTH AFRICA

RED SEA

MECCA

Above. By 1150, the early unified Muslim Empire based on the city of Baghdad was divided into a number of smaller, independent territories.

Lands under Almoravid control

Lands under Fatimid control

Lands under control of the Seljuk Turks

Byzantine Empire

Lands under Ghazenevid control

Right. A page from a 14th century copy of the *Qur'an*. The handwritten text (in Arabic) is ornamented with graceful, flowing patterns and enriched with gold leaf.

The *Prophet* Muhammad, who Muslims respect as a messenger sent from God to show people the right way to live, died in AD 632. Within 150 years of his death, Muslim *Caliphs* ruled over an area stretching from Spain to the Chinese border. They brought with them a distinctive, Islamic, form of government, based on the teachings of the *Qur'an* (which Muslims believe to be God's words, reported by Muhammad), and a faith that was rapidly accepted by hundreds of thousands of people.

THE INTERNATIONAL COMMUNITY OF ISLAM Local customs and practices–such as farming methods, crafts, building styles and costumes–naturally continued much as before in these new Islamic lands. But the peoples who lived there became closely linked to one another in an international Islamic community. This came about through their shared religion, through Islamic laws, and

Left. A group of Muslim travelers, pictured in a 13th century manuscript. Many medieval Muslim people were brave and adventurous travelers; merchants, explorers and geographers have all left accounts of their journeys. Other Muslim people traveled from all parts of the known world on pilgrimage to the holy city of Mecca in Arabia.

Above. Many beautiful buildings survive from medieval Muslim lands. This is the Court of the Lions in the Alhambra palace in Granada, southern Spain. It was built during the 13th and 14th centuries. Muslim palaces were famous for their lovely gardens and for the skill and delicacy with which they were built.

through the Arabic language (which was used for prayers and to write many documents).

Also, the friendships and business contacts Muslims made as they fulfilled their religious duty of going on pilgrimage to the holy city of Mecca encouraged close links. By the year 1100, western Muslim lands along the shores of the Mediterranean were increasingly being attacked. There were clashes between Muslim and Byzantine troops, as well. But whatever the problems faced by Muslim rulers in the west, their power remained secure in the 'Muslim heartlands' of Arabia, the Middle East, Iran and Iraq, north India and central Asia.

THE SELJUK TURKS Muslim power was further strengthened by the arrival, in the 10th and 11th centuries, of the Seljuk Turks. The Seljuks were a group of *nomadic* peoples from central Asia. They settled in the Muslim lands, and took control of many countries. They soon became converted to the Islamic faith and formed a tough, trained fighting force, ready to defend their newfound faith and their newly conquered lands.

FURTHER EXPANSION The Islamic faith, and Islamic forms of government, continued to spread further around the world. Muslim states were established in the islands of the East Indies by 1300. In the 13th century, travelers to China noted that Muslim merchant communities could be found in many major cities there.

In Africa, Muslim travelers and traders journeyed southward across the Sahara, bringing their faith to the peoples of Mali and the neighboring kingdoms. Muslim seafarers introduced Islam to the mining and fishing communities along the East African coast, in present-day Ethiopia, Kenya and Tanzania.

ISLAMIC GOVERNMENT AND SOCIETY

Modern-day Muslim pilgrims making their way on foot around the Ka'ba, or 'House of Prayer' in Mecca, the spiritual center of the Muslim world.

The characteristic Muslim form of government aimed to produce a truly Islamic society. In practice, this meant a society which was governed according to the rules laid down in the *Qur'an*, and which followed the example set by the Prophet Muhammad. But what was life really like for people living under Muslim rule?

First of all, it depended on whether you were a Muslim or not. For devout Muslims, living in a land which was governed according to the teachings of their faith was welcome.

Non-Muslims, especially Christians and Jews, were tolerated and sometimes even encouraged to settle in Muslim lands, and were free to practice their own religion. This was in striking contrast to much of northern Europe, where religious minorities were often cruelly *persecuted*.

LEADERSHIP AND TECHNOLOGY Life for people in Muslim lands also depended on how faithfully rulers followed the teachings of Islam. The *Qur'an* encourages people to worship God, to work, to study, to be charitable and to live in peace. Not all Muslim leaders, however, proved capable or desirous of living up to these ideals.

Many Muslim rulers, though, did spend large amounts of money on projects designed to make life better for all citizens, whatever their religion. Irrigation schemes, safer roads, stronger bridges, clean water supplies and, when necessary, famine relief were provided. Muslim rulers and religious leaders also readily encouraged wealthy individuals to give generously to schools, hospitals, universities, *mosques* and libraries.

Above. Muslim horsemen, pictured galloping, from a 15th century manuscript. Medieval Muslim rulers were famous as patrons of scholarship and book production, and there were universities and libraries in many Muslim cities.

Below. In Persia (Iran), typically Muslim artistic styles mingled with local craft traditions to produce an elegant civilization. This 12th century Persian pottery bowl, with its fine-drawn decoration, shows a prince surrounded by his courtiers.

LIFE FOR ORDINARY PEOPLE For ordinary, uneducated people, the coming of Islam did not introduce great changes into their everyday lives, however much it changed their standards of behavior toward one another, and their religious beliefs.

Muslim peasants continued to labor in the fields. Muslim craftsmen created beautiful carpets, pottery, glassware and metalwork in busy workshops. Muslim merchants and shopkeepers bought and sold their merchandise in noisy, crowded bazaars. Muslim women prepared food, cared for their families, brought up their children and worked as maids or domestic servants.

Like the ordinary people of Europe, Muslim country-dwellers and townspeople everywhere worked hard for their living.

MUSLIM ART AND LEARNING

The madrasa (Islamic college) of Ulug-Beg in Samarkand (in the former USSR), built during the 15th century.

Famous Medieval Muslim Scholars

The medieval Muslim world produced some very learned and influential scholars:

Ibn Rushd lived during the 12th century in Spain and North Africa. He was a lawyer and a judge, and wrote on philosophy, medicine, mathematics, law and theology.

Umar Khayyam lived in 12th century Iran. He is remembered today for his poetry, but was more famous during his lifetime for mathematical and astronomical discoveries.

Nasir Al-Din Tusi worked in Iran, under Mongol rule during the 13th century. He was an expert in geometry and astronomy, and founded a laboratory and observatory with the most precise scientific instruments yet discovered from the Middle Ages.

In many parts of the Muslim world, beautiful buildings, such as mosques, colleges and tombs, survive from the Middle Ages to remind us of the splendid achievements of Islamic civilization. In the same way that Muslim government was based on the Islamic faith, Muslim art and architecture were also strongly influenced by the teachings of the *Qur'an*, and by the simple, religious way of life followed by the Prophet Muhammad and the earliest Muslims.

ISLAMIC DESIGNS Local artistic styles and traditions also had an important part to play. Areas where people had developed particular skills, for example, in weaving carpets or making pottery, continued to produce the goods for which they were famous, but in an Islamic way.

Islam forbids making pictures of any living creature whether a person or an animal. Thus, Muslim artists became very skilled at decorating all kinds of buildings and objects with beautiful geometric patterns and abstract designs. These beautiful Islamic objects were in great demand all over the medieval world. They have been found by archaeologists excavating sites as far apart as Scandinavia and China.

ADVANCES IN LEARNING The *Qur'an* encourages learning, and Muslim scholars were highly respected at home and abroad. They were especially famous for their discoveries in the sciences, in such fields as astronomy, mathematics, navigation, engineering, chemistry, geography and medicine.

They also preserved important scientific manuscripts surviving from the time of the Ancient Greeks. If they had not copied these ancient writings, and made accurate translations of them, a great deal of important knowledge would have been lost.

Both men and women studied, although most medieval Muslim women scholars concentrated on literature, philosophy and religious studies. Some women religious thinkers and *mystics* were famous throughout the Muslim world.

EDUCATIONAL ESTABLISHMENTS Universities, colleges, observatories (for studying the stars) and schools were set up in many Muslim lands, often before similar institutions existed in Europe. One of the Muslim rulers of Baghdad built a special 'House of Learning,' which combined a college for senior students from all over the Muslim world, a scientific observatory and a well stocked library.

Muslim scholars were employed by many non-Muslim rulers who valued their skills. For example, King Roger of Sicily commissioned the Muslim geographer, Al-Idrisi, to compile a world map for him.

Muslim mathematicians and philosophers lectured to crowds of Christian students in Italy and Spain. One Spanish writer complained that the students were forgetting their own culture in their eagerness to listen to these great teachers. The writings of Muslim doctors, like Ibn Sina or al-Razi, were studied by scholars all over Europe, and did a great deal to improve the standards of medical care.

Right. Sometimes, Muslim artists did portray people in their work. This illustration comes from a manuscript produced in Baghdad in 1237. It shows Muslim scholars reading and discussing. They are seated in a library. You can see the books neatly stacked in pigeon-holes in a bookcase in the background of the picture.

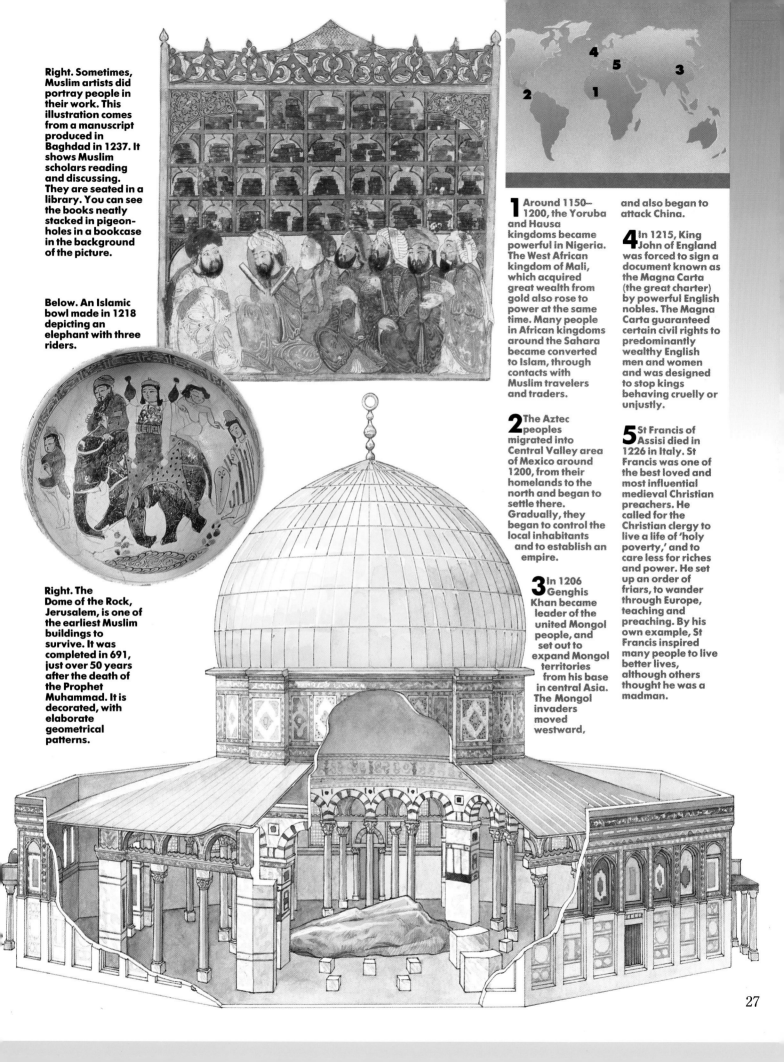

Below. An Islamic bowl made in 1218 depicting an elephant with three riders.

Right. The Dome of the Rock, Jerusalem, is one of the earliest Muslim buildings to survive. It was completed in 691, just over 50 years after the death of the Prophet Muhammad. It is decorated, with elaborate geometrical patterns.

1 Around 1150–1200, the Yoruba and Hausa kingdoms became powerful in Nigeria. The West African kingdom of Mali, which acquired great wealth from gold also rose to power at the same time. Many people in African kingdoms around the Sahara became converted to Islam, through contacts with Muslim travelers and traders.

2 The Aztec peoples migrated into Central Valley area of Mexico around 1200, from their homelands to the north and began to settle there. Gradually, they began to control the local inhabitants and to establish an empire.

3 In 1206 Genghis Khan became leader of the united Mongol people, and set out to expand Mongol territories from his base in central Asia. The Mongol invaders moved westward, and also began to attack China.

4 In 1215, King John of England was forced to sign a document known as the Magna Carta (the great charter) by powerful English nobles. The Magna Carta guaranteed certain civil rights to predominantly wealthy English men and women and was designed to stop kings behaving cruelly or unjustly.

5 St Francis of Assisi died in 1226 in Italy. St Francis was one of the best loved and most influential medieval Christian preachers. He called for the Christian clergy to live a life of 'holy poverty,' and to care less for riches and power. He set up an order of friars, to wander through Europe, teaching and preaching. By his own example, St Francis inspired many people to live better lives, although others thought he was a madman.

27

THE SUNG EMPIRE: WEALTH AND GOOD GOVERNMENT

Sung China After Chin Occupation

KOREA

CHINA

● KAIFENG

● HANGCHOW

EAST CHINA SEA

● CANTON

Sung Empire

Chin Empire

Above. Lands ruled by the Sung Dynasty during the 10th–12th centuries. The northern Sung lands were overrun by the invading Chin dynasty in 1126.

Right. A prosperous Sung couple comfortably seated at table, waited on by their four servants. Vivid tomb paintings like this give us some idea what life was like in Sung China.

The civilization of medieval China astonished every western traveler who came into contact with it. The country and its people seemed amazingly prosperous, energetic, industrious and well governed.

CHINESE PROSPERITY Chinese cities were enormous by medieval standards. For example, Kaifeng, the capital of the Sung Empire, had over a quarter of a million inhabitants in 1120. In comparison, London and Paris housed only a few thousand citizens each. Chinese trade and industry was booming. Workshops and factories produced clothes, furnishings, household goods and porcelain for sale to customers at home and for export to the west, along with spices, drugs and tea.

THE DEVELOPMENT OF TECHNOLOGY The Chinese countryside was crisscrossed by a network of canals, used to transport heavy loads vast distances all over the empire. There were also thousands of irrigation ditches, which provided the water farmers needed to grow high-yielding varieties of rice. These varieties were specially bred by Chinese scientists and gardeners to provide food for the rapidly increasing population.

THE SUNG SYSTEM OF GOVERNMENT Since 907, China had been ruled by the Sung *dynasty*. Like earlier Chinese rulers, the Sung emperors relied on a large number of officials to help them govern the country. In the past, most of these officials had come from wealthy upper-class families. They had been appointed to important posts because of their rank, rather than because of their skills and experience.

Under the Sung, the system of recruitment was changed. Young men who wanted a career in government had to take a difficult examination. If they passed, they were offered a job and thorough training, no matter what their family background was. In this way, the Sung emperors made sure that their government was staffed

1 Around 1100 the first universities were founded in Europe, at Salerno, Bologna and Paris. This was also a great age of cathedral building in many European countries. Building work at Chartres cathedral, France, possibly the finest example of medieval *Gothic architecture*, began in 1154. Architects and craftsmen also designed many strong castles and forts. But in many ways, Europen technologies were less advanced at this time than the Chinese.

2 In 1175 Muhammad of Ghazni (in present-day Afghanistan) expanded his kingdom southward and established the first Muslim empire in India. Muslim influence also expanded at this time in North Africa and the Middle East. In 1189 Saladin led Muslim forces to recapture the city of Jerusalem from Christian Crusaders.

Top. Detail from the Spring Festival Scroll, c.1120, showing a crowded bridge across the river in the Sung capital city of Kaifeng.

Above. An example of skilful Sung engineering, repaired and rebuilt in later centuries — canals and bridges in the walled city of Suzhou, China.

by the most able, intelligent and efficient men in the country. They also encouraged the Chinese people to believe that a career in public service was an honorable and worthwhile way of making a living.

CHINA INVADED All this meant that during the 11th and 12th centuries China was probably the wealthiest and best run state in the world. However, soon this would all change and the Sung emperors and their people would begin to face problems.

Northern China was invaded by the Liao people. The Sung therefore made an alliance with the Chin people, who lived nearby. The Chin helped to defeat the Liao invaders, but then turned to attack the Sung. By 1126, they had occupied about one-third of the Sung territory, including the capital city of Kaifeng. Quickly, the Sung emperors established a new capital at the important trading city of Hangchow, and life in the southern Sung lands returned almost to normal.

CHINA AND JAPAN: CULTURE AND CEREMONY

Japanese medieval temple architecture. This is the impressive gateway leading to the Todaiji Buddhist temple in the city of Nara. It was built during the 8th century.

The Sung emperors, and well educated people who ran their government, valued knowledge, scholarship and the arts very highly. To them, a 'civilized' man or woman was someone who enjoyed music, poetry, painting and philosophy, and could discuss them intelligently. If possible, they were meant to practice these arts, as well. Several of the Sung emperors were skilled painters, *calligraphers* and poets, and they encouraged their *courtiers* and government officials to follow their example.

CODE OF BEHAVIOR These 'civilized' people were expected to behave in a formal and delicate way. Life at the emperor's court was organized in a series of elaborate ceremonies; visitors had to obey a complicated code of polite behavior and good manners. There was friendly rivalry among courtiers over who could write the most elegantly phrased letter, or compose the most fitting poem to celebrate a special day. For some people in Sung China, life itself became a work of art.

LIFE FOR THE RICH Wealthy families collected antiques and precious books, and purchased beautiful paintings by famous artists. Pictures of landscapes were especially liked. These rich patrons also gave money to set up new schools, or to support scholars researching into the relatively long history of Chinese culture, traditions and philosophy.

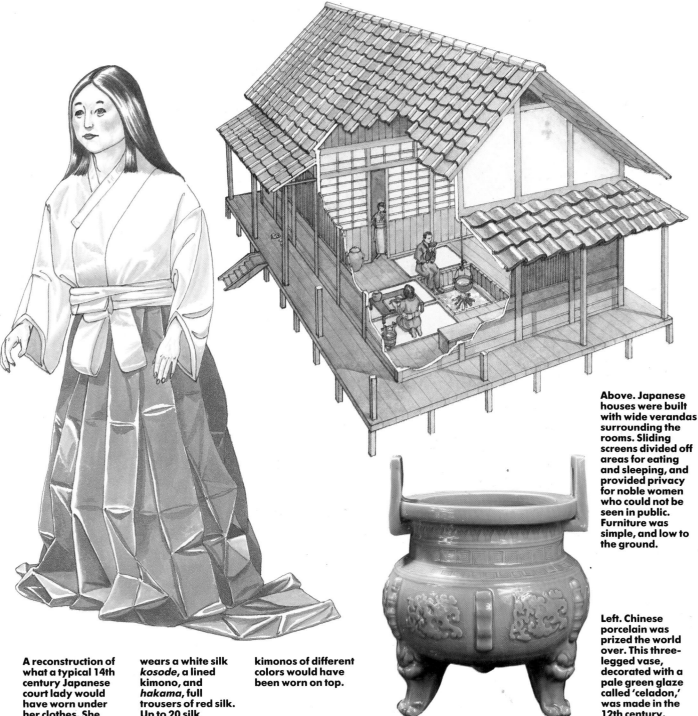

Above. Japanese houses were built with wide verandas surrounding the rooms. Sliding screens divided off areas for eating and sleeping, and provided privacy for noble women who could not be seen in public. Furniture was simple, and low to the ground.

A reconstruction of what a typical 14th century Japanese court lady would have worn under her clothes. She wears a white silk *kosode*, a lined kimono, and *hakama*, full trousers of red silk. Up to 20 silk kimonos of different colors would have been worn on top.

Left. Chinese porcelain was prized the world over. This three-legged vase, decorated with a pale green glaze called 'celadon,' was made in the 12th century.

MUSIC AND PLEASURE Among ordinary people, music and the theater were very popular. At the end of a busy day, everyone enjoyed an outing to the parks, lakes and gardens that were built on the outskirts of the great Chinese cities.

In Hangchow, people could rent a boat and spend a pleasant evening drifting gently across the waters of the great West Lake, listening to music and eating delicious food.

Describing a visit to this spectacularly beautiful lake, Marco Polo (who visited China in the late 13th century) wrote that there was 'more refreshment and delectation (delight) than any other experience on earth'.

INFLUENCE ON JAPAN AND KOREA Chinese culture had a powerful influence on neighboring countries, especially Korea and Japan. Chinese styles of architecture, painting, clothing and writing were admired and copied. A 'Pillow Book' (a sort of diary) written by a Japanese woman courtier has survived from the 10th century. The writer, called Sei Shonagun, frequently quotes Chinese poetry, traditional stories and philosophies, in order to demonstrate to her readers just how refined and civilized she is.

But before the end of the Sung period (around 1279), both Japan and Korea had broken free of Chinese influence, and had turned once more to developing their own national cultures and traditions.

CHINESE INVENTIONS AND DISCOVERIES

The wealthy, well educated, self-confident and energetic Chinese people who lived under the rule of the Sung Dynasty were active merchants and traders. They also sponsored a number of inventions which were far in advance of the technology known in other parts of the world during the Middle Ages.

MATHEMATICS, ASTRONOMY AND GEOGRAPHY

We can group these medieval Chinese inventions and discoveries under several headings: mathematics and astronomy; medical science; weapons and civil engineering; and what we might today call 'information technology.'

To take some examples from each group, in mathematics, Chinese scholars invented new, simple, ways of solving complicated mathematical tasks. They invented a counting board, which worked like a very simple computer. They also worked out a system for doing long division which had not yet been devised.

In astronomy and geography, Chinese scientists developed precision instruments to help them observe the moon and the stars. They also invented a sensitive machine to help predict earthquakes.

MEDICINE

In medical science, Chinese doctors developed the technique of *acupuncture* to control pain and relieve many other symptoms of disease. In addition, through their scientific *dissection* of corpses, they gathered a great deal of valuable knowledge about the human body and how it works. (In the west, the Church forbade the cutting up of dead bodies. It was considered disrespectful to God.)

MILITARY AND CIVIL ENGINEERING

In military engineering, the Chinese invented gunpowder, flamethrowers, poison gas, cannons and tanks. More peacefully, Chinese engineers also invented machines to spin thread, weave cloth, and pump water to irrigate dry land. They extended the already vast system of canals, adding newly designed locks to enable heavily laden cargo ships to sail 'uphill.'

PRINTING

To help the speedy spread of philosophical ideas and, later, practical information, Chinese technologists invented *wood-block printing* sometime during the ninth century. Paper money, which saved merchants from the trouble of carrying heavy loads of gold or silver on their travels, was in use in China by 1024.

THE DECLINE OF NEW INVENTIONS

By 1500, the flow of new Chinese inventions and discoveries seems to have stopped. Why did this marvelous period of invention come to an end? Partly, the prosperity of the country was disrupted by war and invasion. Partly it was due to the rather repressive style of government adopted by the Ming Dynasty, which came to power in 1368. From 1330, the Chinese people were forbidden to carry weapons, and, after 1371, they were barred from traveling abroad. Scholars were encouraged to concentrate on *Confucian* philosophy, rather than on practical subjects, like science and engineering.

But the revolutionary Chinese inventions were not lost or forgotten. Gradually, through contact with Muslim and other traders, Chinese ideas and inventions had been spreading to the west. Many of them, like printing and paper money, are still in use today.

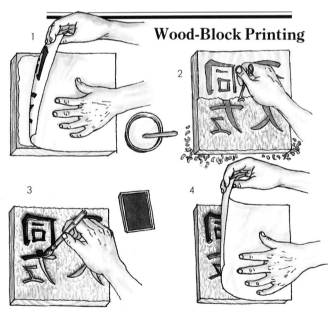

Wood-Block Printing

The drawings above illustrate the processes involved in wood-block printing.

1. Characters were drawn on paper. This was placed upside down on a wood block covered with rice paste, leaving a stain.
2. The paper was removed, and the wood around the stain was cut away.
3. This produced raised characters, which were then inked.
4. Clean paper was pressed onto the inked characters, producing a copy print.

This picture shows mulberry trees being planted by peasants. Mulberry leaves were essential for the Chinese silk industry — they provided food for silk-moth grubs. Silk had been a very early Chinese invention and methods of growing and cultivating developed considerably in order to keep up with demand.

Making Paper Money

Chinese paper was made from pulped fibers from a number of sources – mulberry bark, bamboo shoots and scraps of cloth (1). The bark was first softened (2) then mashed to a pulp (3). Thin layers were then laid over a wide mesh screen. When the layers of pulp were dry, they were removed from the screens, trimmed and pressed to make them as smooth as possible (4). Sheets of paper were printed, using the wood-block method or newer, moveable type. They were then cut into currency notes (5).

Key Dates of Sung and Ming China

907 Collapse of ruling Tang Dynasty, followed by over 50 years of civil war

c.979 Sung Dynasty takes control of large part of former Tang lands, except for regions in the north, which have formed breakaway kingdoms.

1126 The Chin people break their alliance with the Sung and invade Sung lands; Sung power now confined to southern China

1234 Mongol troops attack and overthrow Chin kingdom in northern China

1279 Mongol troops conquer southern (Sung) China. All of China now under foreign control

1340 Series of revolts against foreign rulers by Chinese people

1368 Rebel leader Chu Yuan-chang takes control of large area in southern China, proclaims himself Emperor and establishes new Ming Dynasty

1398 Chu Yuan-chang dies. Yung-lo, his successor as emperor, starts to build new Chinese capital city at Peking (Beijing)

1644 Ming Dynasty overthrown by new ruling family, the Manchu

LIVING IN TOWNS

In the Middle Ages it was unusual to live in a town. Most people, in most parts of the world, lived in the countryside. But the growth in population during the High Middle Ages and the expansion of trade and industry led to an increase in the size and number of towns.

RESOURCES FOR TOWNS Towns depended on the countryside. People living in farmsteads and villages produced food for the townspeople to eat, and raw materials used by craftsmen who lived there. They grew wool, flax, silk or cotton, depending on the local climate and soil, and supplied animal-based products such as leather, horn, bone, fur and feathers.

CENTERS OF TRADE People came to the towns to buy and sell. Some towns had originated as fortresses–safe places where people could shelter from attack–but even these soon developed into trading centers. Craftsmen set up their workshops in the towns, knowing that their goods would be seen and purchased by far more people than in isolated villages.

Professional people, such as lawyers, doctors and scribes, also came to live in the towns, where they knew their skills and services would be needed by many people. Shops and stalls selling food, clothes and household goods were opened to cater to the new town-dwellers. Some towns organized yearly fairs, where traveling merchants from many lands displayed their goods to customers who came from miles around.

ROYAL APPROVAL Kings and princes encouraged the growth of towns in their countries. They knew that taxes and tolls levied on everything that was sold would mean extra income for them. They offered special protection to towns, and to merchants traveling to trade there.

DANGERS OF TOWN LIFE Life in towns was busy, and probably felt very exciting to a visitor used to a quieter life in the countryside. But towns could also be dangerous and unhealthy places to live. Criminals lurked in dark alleys; and diseases bred among the tightly packed shops and houses, and in the refuse cluttering the streets. In contrast, western travelers to Chinese and Muslim towns were greatly impressed by the gardens and orchards that surrounded them. They provided welcome fresh air, peace and relaxation for all the citizens.

Above. The town of Feurs, in the south of France, as it appeared in the early 16th century. The town walls and strong gates protect the inhabitants from enemy armies and from bands of local brigands. Within the walls, the houses are tightly packed together. The church stands in the center of the town, with the houses of the most important citizens nearby. Outside the walls, there are fields, gardens, orchards and a monastery.

The Largest Medieval Cities

These maps show the location of the world's ten largest towns, in 1250 and in 1450. It is not surprising (see pages 20–33) to discover that the great Chinese cities head the list. European cities, like Venice and Paris, remained relatively small in medieval times. In 1250, Venice housed 90,000 people, and Paris 160,000. This is because most people in Europe made their living in the countryside from farming, rather than in towns, from trade or manufacturing.

The 10 largest cities in 1250

1. Hangchow, 320,000
2. Cairo, 300,000
3. Canton, 250,000
4. Nanking, 250,000
5. Fez, 200,000
6. Kamakura, 200,000
7. Pagan, 180,000
8. Sian, 175,000
9. Paris, 160,000
10. Peking, 160,000

Other large cities at this time included:

Constantinople, 150,000
Baghdad, 100,000
Venice, 90,000
Seville, 90,000
Delhi, 80,000
Alexandria, 60,000

The 10 largest cities in 1450

1. Peking, 600,000
2. Vijayanagar, 455,000
3. Cairo, 450,000
4. Hangchow, 360,000
5. Nanking, 350,000
6. Canton, 300,000
7. Tabriz, 200,000
8. Soochow, 200,000
9. Mandu, 200,000
10. Granada, 165,000

Other large cities at this time included:

Samarkand, 100,000
Bruges, 95,000
Damascus, 85,000
London, 75,000
Chan-Chan, 70,000
Lisbon, 66,000

Above. This reconstruction of a street scene in a European medieval town shows many typical features of urban life: crowds, market stalls, shoppers and idle gossips, street musicians and entertainers, watchmen, heavily laden travelers, churchgoers, and straying animals. What it cannot show is the noise, smoke and smells.

INTERNATIONAL TRADE

The waterfront at Venice in the late 15th century. Venice was the finest port in medieval Europe, and a great meeting place for east-west trade.

International trade was well established long before the beginning of the Middle Ages. But the years 1100–1300 saw a great increase in the quantity of goods bought and sold, and in the amount of money made from trading. The growing population in many parts of the world meant that there was an increased demand for all kinds of goods.

BENEFITS OF TRADE FOR RICH AND POOR
High prices for food led to high profits for landowners. They had money to spend on new buildings, and a host of luxury items. Ordinary people never had much money to spare for luxuries, but even they needed to buy basic necessities such as shoes, warm blankets, and sturdy cooking pots from time to time. Everyday goods like these were made locally, but where did all the luxury goods come from? And how did they travel to markets halfway around the world?

THE LUXURY TRADE
Jewelry and spices were the most valuable of all the goods traded. Spices were grown in India and the East Indies, and transported to eager customers in Europe and the Far East. Precious stones came from Burma and India; silk and porcelain (also cheap, mass-produced pottery) from China. The Islamic world produced glassware, metalware and carpets, while Northern Europe supplied fine woolen cloth, amber, furs, metalwork, gold and silverware.

TRADE ROUTES
There were two major networks of international trade routes traveled by adventurous merchants from many lands, and many smaller routes, as well. The 'Silk Road' led overland from European trading ports to the city of Hangchow on the east coast of China. The 'Spice Route' involved travelers in a long voyage by both sea and land. They set off from the Italian ports of Venice and Genoa to Alexandria in Egypt. From there they traveled overland, riding on horses or camels, to the Red Sea or the Persian Gulf. Finally they traveled by ship along the coasts of Arabia or East Africa, and across the ocean to India and the Spice Islands of the East Indies.

Journeys by either route were dangerous, unpredictable, and could take several years. Not many

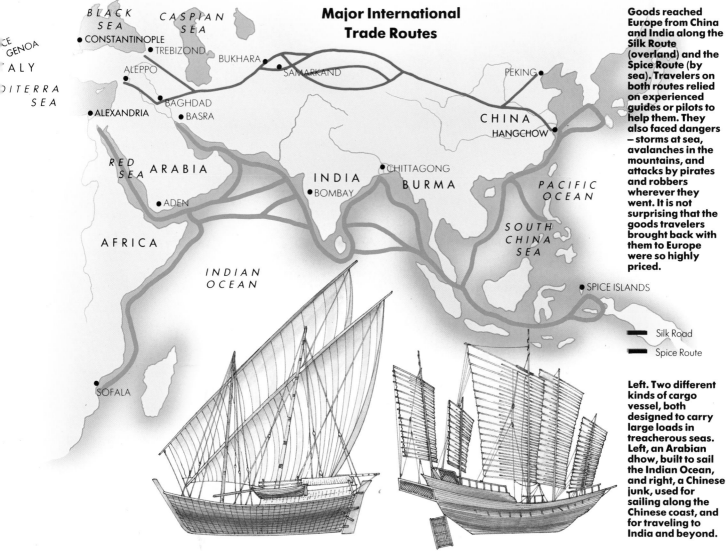

Major International Trade Routes

Goods reached Europe from China and India along the Silk Route (overland) and the Spice Route (by sea). Travelers on both routes relied on experienced guides or pilots to help them. They also faced dangers – storms at sea, avalanches in the mountains, and attacks by pirates and robbers wherever they went. It is not surprising that the goods travelers brought back with them to Europe were so highly priced.

▬ Silk Road
▬ Spice Route

Left. Two different kinds of cargo vessel, both designed to carry large loads in treacherous seas. Left, an Arabian dhow, built to sail the Indian Ocean, and right, a Chinese junk, used for sailing along the Chinese coast, and for traveling to India and beyond.

Medieval Trade

Below the modern historian, Sylvia Thrupp, describes a 15th century shopkeeper in the small English provincial town of Leicester. It shows how much international trade had developed by the end of the Middle Ages:

This man was at the same time draper, haberdasher, jeweler, grocer, ironmonger, saddler and dealer in timber, furniture and hardware. Even this does not describe him adequately, for he had a small stock of wool, wool-fells (fleeces), and skins on his

Money balance, used by merchants and bankers to weigh solid silver coins.

hands, and he could have offered you ready-made gowns in taffeta or silk, daggers, bowstrings, harpstrings, writing paper, materials for making ink, and seeds for the vegetable garden. His resources were greatest in the drapery department, which comprised twenty different kinds of British and imported cloth; he was also well stocked with small wares, notably purses of gold cloth, ribbons, skeins of Paris silk, children's stockings, silk coifs (headscarves) and kerchiefs for nuns.

merchants traveled the whole distance themselves. Instead, they met other traders at well known market centers, like Samarkand and Bukhara in central Asia (in the former USSR), or Constantinople (Istanbul) and Trebizond, on the shores of the Black Sea. There, they bought and sold valuable goods, and exchanged information about prices, opportunities for bargains, and dangers along the route.

MONEY FOR TRADE GOODS Goods were sold for gold and silver coins (which could be weighed to find out their true value) or sometimes for precious stones. Marco Polo mentions sewing sapphires and rubies into the lining of his coat, to provide funds for emergencies. Italian merchant companies based in market towns began to operate as banks, issuing notes of credit (which worked somewhat like a modern credit card). They also loaned money to merchants.

Travelers to China commented on the fact that paper money was widely used among merchants there. But it was a long time before that Chinese invention was copied in the west.

MERCHANTS AND MERCHANDISE

If the risks of long-distance international trade were great, then so were the rewards. Shrewd, successful merchants were among the wealthiest people in many parts of the world. They even loaned money to kings and princes. During the 14th century, the kings of England borrowed huge sums to pay for the costs of their wars with France. Young men enthusiastically offered to work for great merchant families in the hope that they would learn the secrets of how to make money.

TRICKS OF THE TRADE In fact, there were no great secrets to learn. Medieval merchants made their profits because of the scarcity, and, usually, the high quality, of the goods they offered for sale. Spices, silks, jewels and perfumes were very expensive to buy, but they were essential purchases for any noble or wealthy family that wanted to have social standing.

Medieval people–in many lands–were very conscious

Above. Bankers and money-lenders played an important part in medieval trade. Here, we can see medieval bankers counting their stock of gold coins, and locking them safely away in a strong wooden chest.

Left. Travelers in many **Middle Eastern and Asian lands had to pass** through wild, empty countryside, many miles from the nearest town, or village. They stayed at *caravanserais*, like the one shown in this reconstruction drawing. Caravanserais were rest-houses, which provided rooms and food for weary travelers, as well as fodder and shelter for their animals. There was also the opportunity to meet other merchants and travelers, and to gather information about the route that lay ahead. Some caravanserais were provided with bath-houses, which must have been very welcome after days or weeks without the chance to wash.

of appearances. A nobleman and his wife knew they had to dress as well as other nobles or risk losing the respect of people around them. It was also their duty to offer hospitality and entertainment to important people to keep their friendship and, perhaps, to seek their protection and goodwill. Merchants could therefore charge high prices for their produce, because they knew that people simply had to buy them.

ACCOUNTING Successful merchants also kept a close watch on how their business was operating. We know from several surviving letters written by merchants that they worried constantly about prices, arrangements for shipping goods, the dangers of damage or theft, and about lazy employees in their shops and offices. During

When the traveler leaves Kerman (in Iran), he rides for 7 days along a very uninviting road . . . For 3 days he finds no running water, or as good as none. What water there is is brackish and green as meadow grass. MARCO POLO

the Middle Ages, improved systems of accounting were developed, which made it easier for merchants to calculate the profits and expenses on any transaction.

THE SOCIAL WORLD OF MERCHANTS Great merchant families made use of social contacts and arranged marriages between their children to improve business prospects. They knew, also, that generous gifts to charities in their hometowns would make people think well of them. They were careful not to offend local rulers and officials in whatever country they happened to be. They did not want to languish in some foreign prison, or have their goods seized.

Often, merchants played an active part in politics in their native cities. They became town officials, or advisers to the government. In such positions they could make sure that all new laws that were passed increased their chances of making a profit.

Left. Muslim travelers, seated on camels, arrive in a Middle Eastern village. In the background, you can see the mosque, with its dome and minaret. Inside the village houses, the local people are working and talking. A shepherd girl is spinning thread, and watching over her goats who have come to drink at the pond. Scenes like this must have been familiar to many medieval traveling merchants.

Above. Merchants in Europe sold their goods at markets and fairs. One of the most important international fairs was the Lendit fair at Paris, held every year shortly before Easter. This 15th century manuscript shows the Bishop pf Paris (center) blessing merchants who are busy setting up their stalls. Many have arranged their goods under curved, tent-like covers, made of canvas stretched over wooden frames.

Three Great Civilizations
TIME CHART

	EUROPE	MUSLIM WORLD	CHINA AND THE EAST	REST OF WORLD
969		Muslim power established in Egypt; city of Cairo founded		
979			Sung Dynasty reunites Chinese lands	
1000			'Golden Age' of Chinese painting and porcelain	Vikings land in North America. Beginnings of settlement at Great Zimbabwe, Africa
1019	First Russian Kingdom prospers under King Yaroslav I			
1045			Printing with moveable type invented in China	
1055		Seljuks take control of government in Baghdad		
1066	Norman Conquest of England			
1071		Seljuks defeat Byzantine armies at Battle of Manzikert. Byzantine Empire now in danger		
1095	Pope Urban encourages the sending of the First Crusade			
1096>1198		Fighting between Muslim troops and Crusader armies in the lands around Jerusalem		
1100	First universities founded in Europe			Toltec civilization powerful in Central America
1125	German peoples expand their settlement into eastern Europe			
1126			Sung Chinese lands invaded by Chin peoples from the north	
1150			Great Hindu temple of Angkor Wat built in Cambodia	Yoruba states rise to power in Nigeria
1150>1250	Flowering of noble culture celebrating knighthood and chivalry			
1170			Powerful kingdom of Srivijaya flourishes in Java and East Indies	
1175		Muhammand of Ghazni founds first Muslim Empire in India		
1193			Zen Buddhist philosophy established in Japan	
1200				Kingdom of Mali (West Africa) flourishes. Aztec peoples migrate to Mexico
1215	Magna Carta signed; shows kings' powers can be controlled by the people			
1300				Benin kings establish empire in Nigeria

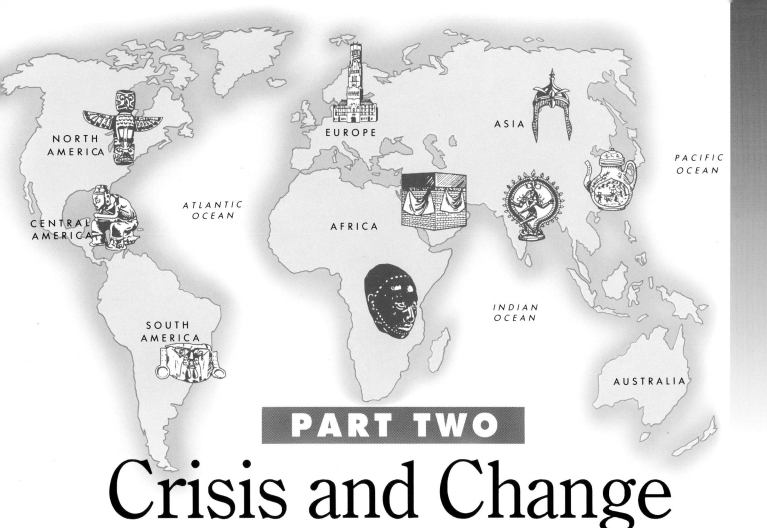

NORTH AMERICA

CENTRAL AMERICA

ATLANTIC OCEAN

SOUTH AMERICA

EUROPE

AFRICA

ASIA

PACIFIC OCEAN

INDIAN OCEAN

AUSTRALIA

PART TWO

Crisis and Change

After 1300, living conditions in many parts of world changed dramatically. Famines, wars, invasions and, worst of all, plague, swept across Europe and many parts of Asia, bringing death and destruction.

THE BLACK DEATH Plague, in particular, had a disastrous psychological effect. People became anxious and depressed. They feared that the world might be coming to an end, or that they were being punished by God for their sins. In Europe, 15th-century preachers suggested that children were killed by the plague because they disobeyed their parents: *it may be that for vengeance of this sin of un-worshipping and despising their fathers and mothers, God slayeth children by pestilence [plague], as you see every day . . . .*

Part Two of this book looks at these catastrophes and examines their effects. It also shows how these disasters were followed by a slow period of recovery, until, by about 1500, life was almost 'back to normal.'

RECOVERY However, the series of disasters had left their mark. The world in 1500 was a very different place from the world 200 years earlier. Old beliefs had been shaken, new governments had seized power, and different ways of fighting, farming and manufacturing had been introduced. In some countries, economic recovery

had brought with it a sense of excitement and possibility, and a wish to explore, question and make discoveries.

In 15th-century Italy, the movement known as the *Renaissance* (re-birth) led to great changes in learning, philosophy and the arts. In Germany, the invention of printing allowed these new ideas to be spread throughout Europe much faster than before.

TRAVEL AND EXPLORATION In the Muslim world, intrepid travelers like Ibn Battuta covered vast distances, recording and commenting on all the sights they had seen. Chinese voyagers journeyed westward to India and beyond, while in Europe, sailors and adventurers sailed southward along the west coast of Africa to try and discover new routes to the rich East.

The most important of these late-medieval discoveries was the accidental landing in America by European explorers in the late 15th century. Although it is incorrect to think of either North or South America as empty, undeveloped land, the realization that there was a vast area of the earth's surface that no-one in Europe or Africa had previously known about had an enormous impact on people living in Europe at the time.

At the same time as many countries and civilizations were recovering from the 14th century crises, they were also developing a whole new way of looking at the world.

Crises and Catastrophes
TENSIONS IN EUROPE

Religious Discontent in Europe

By the end of the Middle Ages, many priests, religious scholars and ordinary people had become dissatisfied with the conduct of the Catholic Church. The 14th century saw a number of political scandals within the Church (including, for a time, two rival popes) which lessened people's respect for the Church as an institution.

Religious protest took several forms. Some people stayed away from Church, others set up illegal, 'alternative' congregations, or circulated forbidden translations of the Bible and other religious books. Their main criticisms and demands were as follows:

● Church government should be reformed.

● There should be

better control of clergymen's personal behavior.

● The Bible should be translated into European languages, that everyone could understand, rather

Left. There was also discontent among priests and their congregations during the late Middle Ages. Martin Luther (1483–1546) the German Protestant reformer, came at the end of a long tradition of demands for reform within the Catholic Church.

than remain in Latin.

● There should be more participation by ordinary people in Church services, and these should be said in everyday languages, rather than in Latin.

● Corrupt practices should be abolished. For example, the selling of 'indulgences' (pardons for sins) for money should be banned.

● There should be freedom to discuss matters of belief without fear of punishment.

In many ways, European society during the Middle Ages was never far from disaster. War, disease, drought, floods and fire could devastate an entire village or town. Thus, although the years 1100–1300 were times of growth and prosperity for many parts of Europe, there were also tensions, difficulties and dangers lying in wait.

AGRICULTURAL CRISIS There were problems connected with farming. As the population increased, new lands had been cleared and planted with crops. Some historians think that by 1300 all the suitable land in western Europe had been taken into cultivation, and there was no more room for expansion. Other historians have suggested that, by 1300, the population of Europe had already grown too large for the land available. In years when harvest yields were below average, there would not be enough food to go around.

There were widespread famines in Europe between 1315 and 1320, caused by a series of very wet summers which caused crops to rot in the fields and animals to sicken and die. The world climate began to change at this time; winters grew longer and summers were shorter and cooler. The period from the 14th–17th centuries is sometimes known as the 'Little Ice Age.'

SOCIAL PROBLEMS There were also problems with the way that medieval European society was organized.

Kings found it increasingly difficult to rule their countries without the cooperation of their subjects which could not always be guaranteed. Thoughtless, cruel or incompetent kings faced rebellion and disorder. During the 15th century, four English kings were deposed by powerful nobles.

Ordinary people also felt bitter and angry. They resented the enormous differences in wealth between the nobles and themselves. In particular, they hated being unfree. Throughout the 14th and 15th centuries, kings in Europe faced open revolt by groups of peasants and by workers in towns. The reasons for each local disturbance differed, though many stemmed from arguments over taxes, land or rent.

Although none of these rebellions succeeded in overthrowing a national government, they helped to weaken landlords' control over the people who worked on their estates. By 1600, except in eastern Europe, most of the people living in the countryside were free.

INTERNATIONAL PROBLEMS Late-medieval (1300–1500) societies were also disrupted by wars between nations, struggles among rival political groups, and by religious discontent. Many people disliked the power and magnificence of important church leaders. Then in the late 1340s, a new disaster struck which was to have a drastic and lasting effect on the population. The *Black Death* arrived in Europe.

ENGLAND

• SLUIS 1340
• CALAIS 1347
• CRECY 1346

• BRÉTIGNY

FRANCE

ATLANTIC
OCEAN

• POITIERS 1356

English territory

French territory

Lands acquired by
the English by 1360

1340 English victories

The Hundred Years War

The war was fought between England and France over the claim by the English kings to be rulers of the southwestern part of France, and their refusal to accept the King of France as their feudal lord. Instead, they regarded themselves as equals, and in 1328 and again in 1337, King Edward III of England went so far as to claim the French crown for himself by right of inheritance. This led to open

England and France were at war for many years during the 14th and 15th centuries over the English kings' claim to rule Aquitaine. This map shows the lands claimed by the English kings, and the sites of some of the most important battles fought between the opposing armies.

conflict, and the war between England and France continued, with pauses and interruptions, for over 100 years, from 1337–1453.

Left. These three pictures from a 13th century manuscript portray scenes from a dream that King Henry II of England (1138–89) is supposed to have had. In fact, they represent every medieval king's nightmare. They show the three most likely causes of trouble within a medieval European kingdom. The top picture shows discontent among the ordinary people. Armed with their farming tools, spades and pitchforks, they have brought copies of the documents on which their rents and labor services are recorded by their lords, to protest to the king about the unfairness of their position. The second picture shows fully armed knights – on whom the king depended for the defense of his country – turning to attack their royal master. The third picture shows bishops and monks – who played a valuable part in the king's government and administration – arguing with the king, instead of carrying out his orders.

THE BLACK DEATH

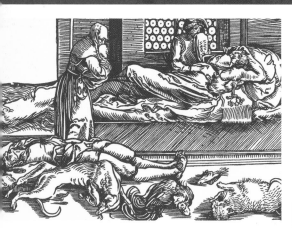

Above. Plague victims, suddenly struck down. From a 15th century German woodcut.

■	1346
■	1347
■	1348
■	1349
■	1350
■	1351
■	1353
■	Barely affected by the plague

BRITAIN

LONDON ●

● PARIS

FRANCE

SPAIN

● CORDOBA

MEDITERRANEAN SEA   ER

NORTH AFRICA

The *Black Death* killed millions– suddenly, swiftly and terribly. Its symptoms were particularly unpleasant: huge, painful swellings, like boils, appeared in the victims' necks, armpits and groins, oozing blood and pus. The sufferer developed a high fever, became delirious, and usually died within 48 hours.

Medieval medicine was powerless to cure the disease, although many strange and curious remedies were tried. People also hoped to protect themselves by

Above. During the 15th century, reminders of death, like this skeleton tombstone from France, appeared in many churches. More comforting images of female saints, especially the Virgin Mary, were also popular.

carrying magic *amulets*, or reciting charms. Priests led weeping processions of *penitents*, beating themselves and praying for deliverance. Some people, more practically minded, washed themselves in herb-scented vinegar, which did, in fact, have powerful antiseptic properties.

HOW THE PLAGUE SPREAD
What was this deadly disease? Most historians think that it was a variety of *bubonic plague*, a serious *bacterial* infection that can prove fatal even today. The plague bacteria were carried in the saliva of blood-sucking fleas, who themselves caught the infection by feeding off plague-ridden rats. When the fleas bit people, the bacteria entered the human bloodstream, where they multiplied rapidly.

A few people were strong enough to fight off the

disease, but, as we have seen, most succumbed within a very short time period.

THE COURSE OF THE PLAGUE
The plague arrived in Europe in 1347. It spread westward from the plains of central Asia, where there was a 'reservoir' of the disease. It soon devastated the entire continent. The Black Death caused tremendous loss of life in the Middle East, North Africa and northern India, as well. Nobody knows exactly how many people perished, but modern estimates suggest that at least a third, and perhaps as many as half, of the total population died.

Deaths were concentrated in areas where people lived close together, especially in towns. The greater density of population made it easier for the disease-carrying rats and fleas to spread. But no one really knew

The Spread of the Black Death

SCANDINAVIA

RUSSIA

NORTH SEA

BALTIC SEA

POLAND

• CRACOW

HOLY ROMAN EMPIRE

HUNGARY

BLACK SEA

• VENICE
• MILAN

CONSTANTINOPLE •

• ROME

N SEA

TURKEY

GREECE

2   1

1 The outbreak of plague in Asia and Far East occurred in 1341. Even though there was widespread loss of life, Chinese rulers went ahead with their plans to expand Chinese territory overseas. In 1349, the first Chinese settlement in Singapore was established.

2 During the 1370s, the great Hindu kingdom of Vijayanagar in India, grew more powerful. It controlled the very profitable spice and cotton trades, and ruled over a large, densely populated territory. Travelers there reported that it was vast (over 7 miles across), strong, and full of beautiful buildings. There were marble palaces, cooling streams, and marvelous gardens. In the north of India, the Muslim Sultanate of Delhi was also rich and powerful. The Sultan held court in great state, and rode in procession with elephants, trumpets and drums.

The Black Death spread westward to Europe and the Middle East from its homeland in central Asia. Only a few remote and sparsely populated areas, such as the highlands of Scotland, escaped. This map shows how rapidly the plague spread, traveling on infected rats in the holds of cargo ships, and then on infected fleas hopping from person to person. Medieval people did not understand how the plague was carried. They thought that strong smells, such as perfumed pomanders or *nosegays*, would drive away the evil plague 'vapors.' But, coincidentally, some medieval housewives may have helped keep disease away from their homes by killing fleas, which nobody liked anyway. Medieval books on housekeeping contain many recipes designed to kill fleas, flies and other insect pests.

When a flea bit an infected rat, it sucked in plague bacteria from the rat's bloodstream. When the flea moved on from rat to human, it injected a minute quantity of rat blood, still **carrying the plague bacteria, into the human bloodstream. Infected humans could also spread bacteria by coughing and sneezing.**

where the plague would next make its deadly attack.

THE CHURCH AND THE PLAGUE Today we understand that the plague is caused by a type of bacteria, but people living (and dying) in the 14th century did not realize this. The fear of death was all around, and even the survivors had to live with horrible memories of suffering and bereavement. Some medieval people saw the plague as another natural disaster, like an earthquake or a flood. Many left their homes and workshops and fled to the remote countryside, hoping to escape infection.

Others shared the Church's view that it was a punishment sent by God, as a result of their wickedness. They gave money to pay for statues, crosses and new church buildings, or commissioned vivid paintings of the torments that awaited sinners in Hell.

The Mongol seige of Baghdad in 1258, from a 13th century Persian manuscript. Even though its power had begun to decline, it was still a major disaster when Mongol troops attacked Baghdad, as part of their campaign to conquer the Middle East. This picture shows the high brick walls and tall watchtowers defending the city, and the splendid buildings crowded within the walls. The Mongol troops, with their tents and horses, are camped outside. They are using a giant catapult to try and smash their way through one of the gates. When the Mongol army finally did make their way into the city, they caused death and destruction. Although medieval casualty figures cannot always be trusted, one contemporary chronicler reporter that over 400,000 people were killed.

The Black Death brought disease and desolation to a large part of the medieval world. But, for people living in India, China, central Asia and the Middle East, it was not the first major disaster to strike their lands. For a long period during the 13th century, whole nations had lived in the fear of *Mongol* attack.

THE ORIGIN OF THE MONGOLS The Mongols were a nomadic people who originated in the harsh *steppe* country of central Asia. They roamed over the vast plains which stretched from Mongolia to the borders of Hungary, seeking good grazing for their flocks and herds. During past centuries they had clashed with more settled civilizations. Most of the time, however, they fought among themselves, since there was fierce rivalry between the different Mongol clans.

GENGHIS KHAN In 1206 the Mongol people became united under one leader, Genghis Khan, and set out to conquer the world. Genghis Khan's ambition was to become 'prince of all that lies between the oceans' (that is, the Pacific and the Atlantic). He very nearly succeeded in his aim. At the time of his death, he was ruler of the largest land based empire the world had ever seen.

THE COURSE OF THE MONGOL ATTACK First the Mongols looked to the east. At this time China was divided into two hostile dynasties: the Chin in the north and the Sung in the south. In 1211 the Mongols invaded the Sung Empire, and they captured the most important northern city of Peking (Beijing) in 1215. Next they moved westward to attack the Muslim kingdom of

Left. Genghis Khan (c. 1162–1227) sitting in his richly decorated tent. He is surrounded by courtiers, including his sons Jochi and Ogedei. The yak tails flying outside the doorway were a traditional Mongol symbol of authority. From a 13th century Persian manuscript painting.

Mongol Military Techniques

Below. Mongol invasions during the 13th and early 14th centuries. Mongol troops poured westward across the desolate central Asian plains, toward the rich trading cities of the Middle East.

→ Campaigns under Genghis Khan

→ Campaigns under later Mongol leaders

Routes of the Mongol Attack 1219–1260

MONGOLIA
KARAKORUM
PEKING
KIEV
HUNGARY
MEDITERRANEAN SEA
BUKHARA
CHINA
AIN JALUT
BAGHDAD
KABUL
ARABIA
MECCA
INDIA

'[The Mongols] are more numerous than ants or locusts . . . detachment after detachment arrived, each like a billowing sea.'
JUVAINI, A PERSIAN HISTORIAN

All Mongol soldiers were well equipped with bows and arrows, and well supplied with fast, easily-maneuverable horses. They could cover up to 96 miles a day.

They used traps and false ambushes to cause panic among enemy troops, or to lure them to destruction. And they imposed a reign of terror on all the lands they captured. Anyone who dared fight against them was mercilessly killed.

Kwarazim (now in Uzbekistan, part of the C.I.S.). They captured the great trading city of Bukhara in 1220, and burnt it to the ground. Over 30,000 inhabitants were brutally murdered.

The Mongols took few prisoners, preferring to slaughter anyone who opposed them. This cruelty shocked medieval chroniclers, who described the Mongols as bloodthirsty monsters, lacking all human feelings and delighting in death and destruction.

Genghis Khan died in 1227. His son, Ogedei, who ruled after him, first conquered the Chin people in northern China, and then turned to attack Europe. Mongol armies advanced into Russia, where they destroyed the capital city of Kiev in 1240 and continued westward into Hungary. Ogedei died in 1241, and his army retreated. Europe was spared.

CHINA AND THE MIDDLE EAST The Mongol rulers after Ogedei preferred to concentrate their attacks on the Sung Empire in China, and on the Muslim lands of the Middle East. The Muslim capital of Baghdad was attacked in 1258, and, for a time, it looked as if the Muslim holy cities of Mecca and Medina in Arabia would also be captured.

But once again, the Mongol forces retreated. Soon, another invasion was planned, but the Mongol troops were defeated by a Muslim army at the battle of Ain Jalut (in present-day Israel) in 1260.

After more than 50 years of terror and bloodshed, the Mongol threat to Islam had disappeared. China was not so fortunate. The Sung people fought valiantly against repeated Mongol invasions, but were finally defeated.

THE RESULTS OF THE MONGOL INVASIONS

Genghis Khan (center) with his descendants, including Babur, who founded a new ruling dynasty in India.

Key Dates of the Mongol Invasions

The Mongol Empire in the 13th century

1206	Genghis Khan unites the Mongol people under his leadership and prepares for world conquest
1211–1215	Mongols attack China
1227	Genghis Khan dies
1229	Ogedei Khan proclaimed new Mongol leader
1234	Ogedei's generals capture northern China
1240	Russian capital city of Kiev captured
1258	Important Muslim city, Baghdad, captured
1260	Kublai elected Great Khan
1279	Mongol troops overthrow Chinese southern Sung Dynasty
1294	Kublai Khan dies; Mongol power declines
1336–1405	Mongol power temporarily revives under Timur. After Timur's death, the era of Mongol danger is over.

Although *Mongol* armies vanished from western lands, Mongol conquests in the east continued. Sung China was overrun in 1279 by an army led by Kublai Khan, who ruled from 1260 to 1294. Kublai Khan was less bloodthirsty than some of his ancestors. He was intelligent, curious and interested in philosophy. But he still went to war. He sent two separate battle fleets to try and capture Japan, in 1274 and 1281, but they were both defeated. The Japanese said that the gods had sent a 'divine wind' from heaven to drive the Mongols away.

THE ACHIEVEMENTS OF KUBLAI KHAN Kublai Khan used the riches from his Chinese conquests to pay for a mighty army. He did not destroy the rich Chinese trading cities, but exploited their wealth and enjoyed the comfortable lifestyle they offered. Marco Polo, who worked for Kublai Khan and admired him, called him 'the most powerful man since Adam.' But Kublai Khan's

empire did not last long after his death. By the 1360s Chinese rebels had overthrown their Mongol conquerors, and established a new ruling dynasty, the Ming, which governed the Chinese people for the next 300 years.

EFFECTS OF THE MONGOL INVASIONS In the short term, the nations which Mongol armies attacked suffered terribly. Hundreds of thousands of people were killed. The Muslim historian, Ibn al-Athis, reckoned that it was the greatest disaster humanity ever had to endure. Prosperous cities, full of fine houses and graceful mosques were destroyed. Many rare books, works of art, scientific instruments and precious jewels were smashed or looted. Fields and orchards lay neglected and full of weeds; the men and women who worked in them fled in terror as they heard of the Mongol approach.

In the long term, the Mongols achieved very little of

The Career of Genghis Khan

In 1206, Temujin, a Mongol prince, was proclaimed leader of all the Mongol peoples at a great assembly. He went on to take the name, Genghis Khan, which means 'Prince of all that lies between the oceans.' He devoted the rest of his life to conquest, death and destruction.

He died in 1227 in China 'without regrets.' His body was carried from China to his homeland in Mongolia with great ceremony. Every living creature met by the funeral procession was killed so that it might serve Genghis Khan in the next world.

Left. Genghis Khan's funeral procession which carried his body from China, where he died, aged 73, to his ancestral homeland in Mongolia.

Tomb of the Mongol leader, Timur, in Samarkand, C.I.S. Timur became a Muslim; his tomb is built in an Islamic style.

lasting importance. But, in spite of their appetite for death and destruction, they did manage to bring peace, of a sort, to many parts of Asia for over 100 years. Once lands were under Mongol control, feuds between local chieftains which made overland travel so dangerous for merchants came to an end.

THE MONGOLS UNDER TIMUR The 'Mongol Peace' vanished soon after the collapse of Mongol power in China. But the threat of Mongol attacks did not completely disappear for another 100 years. Under their leader Timur (sometimes known as Tamburlane), Mongol armies clashed with Muslim forces in Turkey. Timur had the defeated Muslim commander, Sultan Bayezid, paraded round his court in a cage.

But Timur, although savage, was different from earlier Mongol leaders. He abandoned the tribal beliefs and the *nomadic* way of life of his ancestors. He became a Muslim, and seems to have appreciated city life. He rebuilt his capital city of Samarkand with many beautiful mosques, elegant tombs and lovely gardens.

Recovery
EUROPE: PROSPERITY RENEWED

The *Black Death*, and the repeated outbreaks of *plague* during the 14th and 15th centuries, had an unexpected side effect. Many of the survivors grew richer. How did this happen?

CHANGES IN WORKING CONDITIONS At first, farming, trade and industry all suffered as the plague devastated towns and villages. But soon, merchants, craftsmen and farm laborers were back at work. There were, however, important differences from life in the old days. Before the Black Death, there had been plenty of workmen available. Some historians even think there were too many workers, and that some were unemployed. This meant that wages were low, and working conditions were poor. Masters in the towns and in the countryside knew that they could always find men and women desperate for work.

The plague changed all that. Since so many people had died, workers were now in short supply. Wages rose, and workmen felt free to move from job to job, seeking better pay. At the same time, prices for basic necessities, like food and fuel, were reduced. The smaller population meant that there was less demand for them. With higher wages, and a

Left. Portrait of the German merchant Georg Gizse, painted by Hans Holbein in 1532.

Europe After the Plague

After the Black Death had disappeared, many people tried to reason why it had occurred. Fifteenth century preachers thought that the repeated attacks of plague (which killed mostly young people, who had not developed a resistance to the plague bacteria) were sent from God to punish disobedient children. Here are the reasonings of one preacher:

it may be that [for] vengeance of this sin of un-worshipping and despising of fathers and mothers, God slayeth children by pestilence, as you see every day, for in the old law, children that were rebels and unbuxom to their fathers and mothers were punished by death . . .

Merchant cities in northern Europe grew rich on the profits of trade. In particular, ports along the shores of the Baltic and the North Sea flourished and prospered. Many, like King's Lynn in eastern England, or Bruges in Belgium, spent money on fine new buildings. This photograph of Rothenburg, in northern Germany, shows substantial merchant houses of the type built during the later Middle Ages.

lower cost of living, workers now had money left over to spend.

Some bought or rented bigger houses or more land; others chose to purchase better quality food, or finer clothes. Governments passed laws to try and stop this, feeling that rich foods and fashionable clothes were only fit for nobles. But they were not very successful.

PROSPERITY How did all this affect other members of society? Merchants and craftsmen welcomed the extra money that workers had to spend. And, as their businesses expanded, they, too, made more money. As the number of people in Europe gradually increased, merchants and craftsmen prospered still further, and took on more workmen to help them produce more goods.

HARD TIMES FOR LANDLORDS Almost the only people in medieval Europe who did not grow more wealthy as a result of the plague were landlords. If they wanted workers to harvest their crops, they had to pay high wages. But they knew that the corn they took to market would not sell at a very high price. Their profits were disappearing. What could they do?

Some landlords leased their fields to farmers in return for a low income. Some let fields return to woodland or waste. Others, especially in England, gave up growing corn and raised sheep instead. Wool still sold at a good price, and sheep needed few workers to look after them. Harsh landlords tried to force people who rented houses and plots of land to do all their farm work for them, as they had during the 11th and 12th centuries. But workers simply left these lords' estates, and found a better place to live elsewhere.

Right. A reconstruction drawing of the magnificent market hall at Bruges in Belgium, built during the 15th century to bring honor and prestige to the town. It is topped by a spectacular tower, built in a flamboyant Gothic style.

Merchant Cities

Another confident civic building – the Town Hall at Bruges, in Belgium, built during the 15th and early 16th centuries.

Towns and cities in northern Europe, especially in Belgium and northern France, grew rich on the profits of buying and selling. The most prosperous towns were connected with the cloth trade. They made their money by importing fleeces and yarns, then weaving, dying and finishing fine woolen fabrics. Rural areas, like the Cotswold hills of England, where sheep were raised to produce high quality fleeces, also grew rich.

The picture was not so rosy for some southern European cities. Plagues, wars and bad debts all led to a slowing down of trade within the Mediterranean area. Although individual merchant families managed to make good profits throughout the economic depression, other businesses in Italy and southern France found their profits decreasing.

THE RENAISSANCE

Even though many parts of Europe prospered during the later 14th and 15th centuries, many people must still have been miserable and frightened. Most families knew someone who had died of the plague. Worse still, nobody really understood how the disease spread, and so people lived in the constant fear that soon it might be their turn to die.

As a result, many religious brotherhoods and sisterhoods were formed. Many beautiful paintings, statues, prayer books and other works of art on religious subjects were given to churches. Wandering preachers thundered out their message to packed congregations, urging them to abandon their sinful lives.

THE BEGINNING OF THE RENAISSANCE However, at the same time as all this intense religious activity, a new, confident and non-religious way of looking at the world was emerging. The *Renaissance* (it means 'Re-birth'), as this movement was called, began as a collection of artistic and philosophical ideas. They first became popular in Italy, but were soon discussed by artists and scholars all over Europe.

A NEW LOOK AT THE WORLD Renaissance painters, sculptors, teachers and thinkers combined a keen interest in the remains of ancient Greek and Roman culture with the wish to create something totally new. They abandoned the old medieval styles of painting and writing. Instead, they tried to show the world with scientific accuracy. They studied the human body, plants, rocks and animals, and experimented with new ways of drawing, so that they could reproduce 'real' landscapes and 'real' people in their pictures. They examined ancient statues and carvings, to learn from the skills of artists who had lived hundreds of years ago.

THE IMPORTANCE OF PRINTING Renaissance scholars also studied Greek and Roman texts, and translated, edited and printed them so that the ideas they contained could become widely understood. Printing, which was invented in Germany during the 15th century (although a similar system had been known in China for many years), was very important in spreading Renaissance ideas

Italian City States in the 13th and 14th Centuries

- VENICE
- MILAN
- GENOA
- BOLOGNA
- FLORENCE
- SIENA
- PAPAL STATE
- ROME
- ADRIATIC SEA
- KINGDOM OF NAPLES AND SICILY
- TYRRHENIAN SEA

Italy was not a unified country at the time of the Renaissance. Instead, it was divided into many smaller city states, usually consisting of a busy town and the fields and farms surrounding it. Some of these city states were rich and powerful, like the great ports of Venice and Genoa. Others were small and impoverished. Wars were frequent among the Italian states.

throughout Europe. Many Renaissance artists and philosophers lived as Christians. But for others, the newly available Greek and Roman ideas, and their own observations from nature, led them to challenge the teachings of the Church. Some, like the astronomer Galileo, were even prepared to die for their beliefs.

PATRONAGE Who paid for all this artistic and scholarly activity? Wealthy patrons demanded new buildings, paintings, sculptures and books, all produced in the Renaissance style. Kings, nobles and city governments competed with one another to employ the most skilful artists, and the most intelligent philosophers. Powerful men and women became interested in Renaissance ideas, and in discussing what made the ideal Renaissance society.

Thus, the Renaissance changed Europe in several ways.

Key Figures of the Italian Renaissance

Filippo Brunelleschi (1377–1446) was an architect who studied Ancient Roman buildings and sculpture. He built the dome of Florence cathedral in classical Roman style.

Piero della Francesca (1420–1492) perfected the art of perspective drawing. This was an important Renaissance technique which enabled painters to depict space accurately and realistically in their works.

Marsilio Ficino (1433–1499) was a Renaissance *humanist* who studied the writings of Ancient Greek and Roman philosophers. He believed that human achievements, rather than God's will, could bring about a 'golden age' of peace, beauty and goodwill.

Sandro Botticelli (1444–1510) was a painter who combined traditional Christian religious subjects with Renaissance humanist ideas. The style of his paintings was greatly influenced by Ancient Greek and Roman art.

Leonardo da Vinci (1452–1519) was a painter, scientist, military engineer and inventor. He studied human anatomy and the world of nature, and portrayed them accurately in his works. He designed many extraordinary machines, including a submarine and a helicopter.

Niccolo Machiavelli (1469–1527) was a writer on politics, who offered advice to Italian Renaissance princes. He is famous for suggesting that, in politics, 'the end justifies the means'. That is, any methods, however unpleasant or unlawful, should be considered when planning effective political action.

Michelangelo Buonarotti (1475–1564) was a painter, sculptor and poet and is famous for his paintings decorating

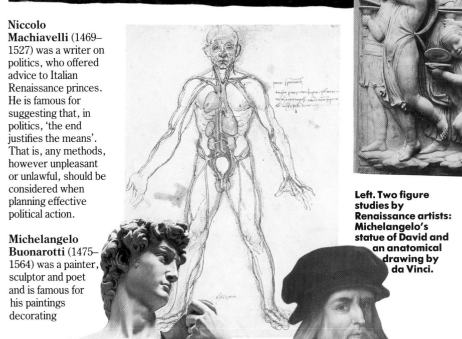

Left. Roman art, from the second century BC. A carved marble tomb, showing a mythological scene.

Below. Renaissance art, imitating Roman designs. A carving by the Italian artist, Luca della Robbia, in Florence Cathedral, c. 1438. Della Robbia used a pagan style over 1500 years old to decorate a 'new' Christian building.

Left. Two figure studies by Renaissance artists: Michelangelo's statue of David and an anatomical drawing by da Vinci.

Left. An engraving of Michelangelo. He was one of the greatest artists of the Renaissance.

Above. A self portrait by Leonardo da Vinci. He was one of the most extraordinary and talented figures of the Renaissance.

the ceiling of the Sistine Chapel, in Rome. His work displays his belief in the nobility, beauty, freedom and power of humanity.

Raphael (1483–1520) was a painter who combined portrayals of traditional Christian subjects, with a typically Renaissance realistic technique based on Ancient Greek and Roman models.

Galileo Galilei (1564–1642) was a scientist and professor at the University of Padua. He dared to claim that the earth and the planets orbited round the sun, in defiance of the Church's teaching.

RESTORING ISLAM: THE OTTOMAN EMPIRE

A French 15th century view of the city of Constantinople. The artist, who had obviously never been there, pictured it as a western European city.

While the Renaissance was taking place in Europe, there was revival and recovery in the Muslim world, as well. Some parts of the old Muslim empire—Egypt, Syria, Spain and North Africa—had escaped the Mongol invasions, and survived as peaceful centers of the Muslim way of life. As we saw on page 46, the Muslim holy cities of Mecca and Medina had also been saved from destruction.

In all these places, Muslim scholars, scientists and philosophers continued the Muslim tradition of learning and discovery. In the towns, Muslim craftsmen continued to produce splendid objects in metal, pottery and glass.

But the political strength of the great Muslim Empire, which was already weakened and threatened by rival *sultanates* in many parts of the Muslim world, had been destroyed for ever by the Mongol invasions. By the middle of the 14th century, however, a new Muslim world power–the Ottoman Empire–was beginning to emerge.

UTHMAN As the Mongols retreated, their authority had been replaced by a number of small Muslim states. One of these states was led by Uthman (which became 'Ottoman' in medieval English), a Turkish chieftain who lived from 1281–1324. During his lifetime, Uthman led Muslim troops on campaigns to capture the territories that surrounded his little kingdom.

OTTOMAN EXPANSION The *sultans* who ruled after Uthman continued this policy of expansion. In 1326 Ottoman troops captured the important Byzantine city of Bursa, close to the Black Sea, which became the Ottoman capital. By 1400, the Ottomans controlled a huge area. In 1453, they captured the Byzantine capital city of Constantinople (Istanbul). This brought an end to the Byzantine Empire, and caused a ripple of fear to run across Europe. Where would the Ottomans attack next?

Ottoman conquests continued throughout the 15th and 16th centuries. Under one of their most famous leaders, Sultan Suleiman the Magnificent, the Ottomans advanced eastward, to capture the old Muslim capital of Baghdad. In the west, they controlled the lands known today as Bulgaria, Greece, Albania, Yugoslavia and Hungary. By 1520, they also controlled the once-powerful Muslim states of Egypt and Syria, as well as Mecca, Medina, and the wealthy trading port of Aden in Arabia.

THE OTTOMAN SYSTEM OF GOVERNMENT Like earlier Muslim governments, the Ottomans treated conquered peoples fairly and well. They employed the most capable people they could find–whatever their faith–to help them run their empire. They also used Christian troops, the *Janissaries*, to help them fight their battles. They recruited clever Christian boys to serve in their administration. Also like earlier Muslim rulers, the Ottoman sultans spent a great deal of money on encouraging the arts. Many grand and beautiful mosques were built on the orders of Ottoman rulers.

The Ottoman Empire in 1566

BLACK SEA

GREECE • CONSTANTINOPLE
• BURSA

TURKEY

• BAGHDAD

• TUNIS

PERSIAN GULF   PERSIA

SYRIA

MEDITERRANEAN SEA

NORTH
AFRICA

• SUEZ

EGYPT   ARABIA

RED SEA

• MECCA

• ADEN

Below. The Ottoman empire in 1566. The empire had been greatly expanded during the brilliant reign of Sultan Suleiman the Magnificent (1520–1566). Now it covered over a million square miles, and was a major world power.

1 The Italian Renaissance was at its height from 1400–1500. Important new developments occurred in painting, sculpture, architecture and science. Also, the first printed book in Europe was produced in 1445, by Johannes Gutenberg, in Germany. Painters of the 'Northern Renaissance,' like Memling, van Eyck and Holbein, were active in Belgium, northern France and England. There was a final flowering of Gothic architecture as the Cologne Cathedral, and King's College Chapel, Cambridge, were built during this period.

2 From 1470–1520, the Inca peoples in South America conquered the neighboring Chimu kingdom and began to establish an empire. The Aztec Empire was very powerful in Mexico. These empires were soon to end; in 1492 Christopher Columbus crossed the Atlantic Ocean and made probably the first European contact with American peoples for almost 500 years.

Above. Muslim astronomers studying the stars, and geographers studying a globe, from a 16th century Persian manuscript.

Right. The Ottoman leader, Sultan Mehmet II 'the Conqueror,' who ruled the Ottoman Empire from 1451–1481.

CHINA AND JAPAN: CONSTRUCTION AND DESTRUCTION

The most successful Chinese rebel leader against the Mongols was Chu Yuan-chang (1328–1398). He became the first emperor of the new Ming dynasty. The Ming emperors quickly began the task of reconstruction after the Mongol invasions. New canals and irrigation ditches were dug; the ancient Great Wall of China (originally designed to protect the country against Mongol attacks) was strengthened and repaired; and the war-torn city of Peking was rebuilt. The Ming emperors made it their new capital, and constructed a huge, secret palace (the 'Forbidden City'), to be a home for themselves, their families, and the royal court.

NEW WARS The Chinese emperors soon had to fight to defend their new freedom. Mongol troops launched repeated attacks from the north, and pirate raids became an increasing danger to ships and coastal cities in the south. There were wars, too, when some of the more ambitious Ming emperors tried to conquer new territories. Chu's son, the emperor Yung-lo, tried

Japanese Ceremony

The Samurai's elaborate costume was designed to display his warrior status and to protect him in battle. In medieval Japan, everyday activities, like washing and dressing, could become surrounded by elaborate ritual in royal or noble homes.

This extract comes from the 'Pillow Book of Sei Shonagun' and shows how highly developed simple ceremonies had become. It was written by a female courtier who lived in a Japanese imperial palace during the 10th century. She describes an early morning scene:

Now the attendants brought water . . . As I recall there were altogether six attendants – two young maids and four servants of lower rank . . . The young attendants looked very pretty in their loose, cherry-colored coats; I enjoyed watching them take the basin of water from the servants . . . [The ladies in waiting, who were also taking part in the ceremony] wore divided skirts of green and shaded material, Chinese jackets, waistband ribbons and shoulder sashes; their faces were heavily powdered. The servants passed them what was needed for the washing and I was pleased to see how everything was done with proper ceremony in the Chinese style.

The diagrams above show the many garments that made up the Samurai's battle dress. The ritual of arming could take a long time because he first bathed and perfumed himself so that if he died he would smell sweet.

unsuccessfully to capture Vietnam, and sent huge fleets to demand tribute from rulers in Southeast Asia, India and Sri Lanka.

LIFE IN THE COUNTRYSIDE

For ordinary people in the Chinese countryside, life was still hard work, although the new canals and irrigation schemes helped to increase rice production. Chinese peasants had some machines to help them, unlike farmworkers in western lands. Foot-powered threshing machines, for example, made the task of separating grains of rice from the stalk much easier.

INCREASES IN PRODUCTION

Since the population was increasing rapidly, there was a constant need to clear more land for farming, and to grow bigger and better crops. Farm workers who grew tea and tended silkworms were also kept busy, meeting the demands of foreign customers who were eager to buy these Chinese products. In factory areas, pottery was mass produced, cheaper, basic goods for everyday use at home and abroad, and fine, fragile wares for the luxury trade.

JAPAN: THE WARRING STATES

Japan was never invaded by the Mongols, and remained independent throughout the period from 1100–1500. But the years 1350–1600 were a time of unrest and disorder, often known as the *Warring States Period*. Rival groups of noblemen, each with their own highly trained private army, struggled to gain control of the country.

In spite of these wars, Japanese culture–especially religious thought–flourished and developed at this time. Most Japanese people followed the *Buddhist* faith. During the 12th and 13th centuries, one particular branch of Buddhism–known as *Zen*–became very popular, especially among the noble warriors and their troops.

Beautifully finished pottery was made in specialist centers throughout the country during this period. Solemn, polite, careful ceremonies, based on everyday actions like making tea, but also containing a religious or philosophical meaning, became an important part of upper-class Japanese life at this time.

Above. The Great Wall of China, begun in AD 221 and extended and rebuilt by the Ming emperors. It also provided a powerful symbol of the wealth and resources of the new Ming Empire. The wall runs for over 14,400 miles through rugged countryside, from the Pacific coastline to the deserts and plains of central Asia. There are guardhouses and watchtowers at regular intervals, so that soldiers stationed at the wall could give early warning of an enemy approach.

Above. The Golden Pavilion, or Kinkaku-ji, Japan, built as a country house and monastery by the Japanese Shogun (ruler) Askikaga Yoshimitsu in 1397. The pavilion is surrounded by beautiful gardens and looks over a peaceful lake.

Right. Emperor Chu Yuan-chang, founder of the Ming Dynasty. He was born into a peasant family and won fame as a warrior.

Lands Beyond the Sea
VOYAGES TO THE INDIES

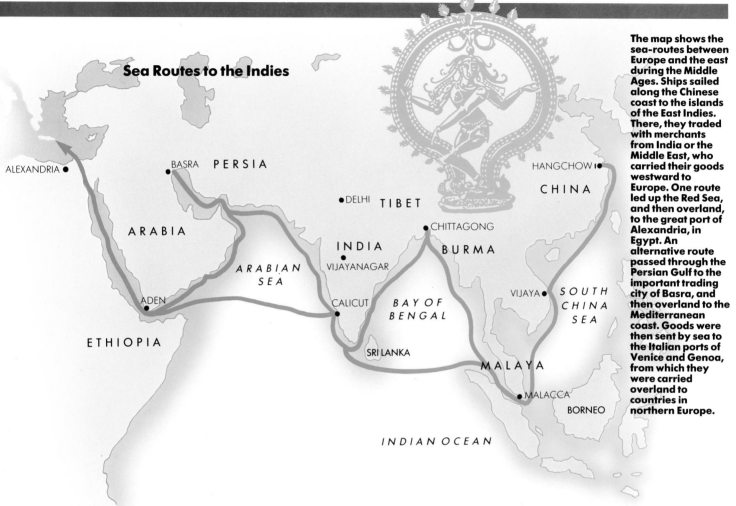

Sea Routes to the Indies

ALEXANDRIA

PERSIA

BASRA

DELHI TIBET

ARABIA

ARABIAN SEA

INDIA

VIJAYANAGAR

ADEN

CALICUT

BAY OF BENGAL

ETHIOPIA

SRI LANKA

CHITTAGONG

BURMA

HANGCHOW

CHINA

VIJAYA SOUTH CHINA SEA

MALAYA

MALACCA

BORNEO

INDIAN OCEAN

The map shows the sea-routes between Europe and the east during the Middle Ages. Ships sailed along the Chinese coast to the islands of the East Indies. There, they traded with merchants from India or the Middle East, who carried their goods westward to Europe. One route led up the Red Sea, and then overland, to the great port of Alexandria, in Egypt. An alternative route passed through the Persian Gulf to the important trading city of Basra, and then overland to the Mediterranean coast. Goods were then sent by sea to the Italian ports of Venice and Genoa, from which they were carried overland to countries in northern Europe.

Some of the most important medieval sea routes were centered on the Indian Ocean, the Bay of Bengal, and the South China Sea. Sailors used seasonal winds (the monsoons) to carry them from Arabia and East Africa to India, Sri Lanka and the islands of the East Indies. When the winds changed, as they did after a few months, they sailed home again, loaded with cargo from distant ports. What were these eastern lands like, and why did sailors risk their lives to get there?

INDIA From the 10th century, most of northwestern India had been ruled by Muslim princes. Among the most famous of these was Muhammad of Ghazni (998–1003), who, like so many Muslim rulers, encouraged poets, scholars, artists and scientists to come to his court. Another powerful Muslim kingdom in India was the Sultanate of Delhi, which was established in 1206.

In earlier years, India had been the home of a brilliant

Eastern Spices

Medieval people liked to use eastern spices to flavor their food. Here is a 15th century recipe for cooking beefsteak or venison:

'Take venison or beef, slice it and fry it until it is brown; then take vinegar and a little *verjus* and a little wine, and add ground pepper and powdered ginger, cook together to make a sauce; when it is ready to serve, scatter powdered cinnamon on top.'

GINGER

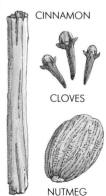

CINNAMON

CLOVES

NUTMEG

Above are shown some of the spices brought back from the East.

Right. An impressive temple chariot, carved in stone, and decorated with statues of Hindu gods and goddesses. From the ruined Vitthala temple in the great Indian city of Vijayanagar.

Left. Part of the magnificent temple buildings at Madura, southern India, dating from the 10th century. Each side of the building is covered with elaborate carvings, showing scenes from Hindu religious epics.

Right. A procession of warriors, war-horses and elephants from a carved stone frieze in the Hazara Rama (king's private temple) in the Indian city of Vijayanagar.

Hindu civilization, ruled over by the Gupta kings. Scientists working then made important discoveries, and Indian philosophers were so famous that Chinese scholars traveled thousands of miles to talk with them. But by 1100, the Gupta Empire had collapsed. Southern India (along with present-day Burma, Thailand, Cambodia, Malaysia, Indonesia and the islands of the East Indies) was divided into small, independent kingdoms. They were linked by shared religious traditions (Hindu and Buddhist) and busy international trade.

TRADE GOODS FROM THE EAST In these lands, ordinary peoples' lives were based on farming and producing goods for sale. Many of these were valuable. Cotton, perfume, pearls, rubies, medicines, dyes and elephants came from India. Malaysia exported tin and timber; the islands, especially Java and Sumatra, grew

pepper and spices. Hardwood trees were cut from forests in Burma and Thailand.

Over the years, some of these trading kingdoms grew rich and expanded, while others declined. All of them left behind wonderful temples and shrines– monuments to their peoples' beliefs and to the wealth of the kings who built them.

THE VIJAYANAGAR EMPIRE Toward the end of the Middle Ages, a new and powerful Hindu empire began to rule over southern India, and to control the profitable spice and cotton trades. Travelers reported that its capital city, Vijayanagar, had half a million inhabitants, was seven miles wide, and was surrounded by seven city walls, one inside the other. The mighty Vijayanagar Empire, however, had a relatively short life and only lasted until 1565, when it was overthrown by armies from north India.

SOUTH OF THE SAHARA

A page from the *Catalan Atlas*, produced for King Charles V of France in 1375. This extract shows Mansa Musa, ruler of the wealthy African kingdom of Mali, holding a gold coin.

During the Middle Ages, Africa was the home of a number of wealthy and thriving civilizations. In several different parts of the continent, powerful kings ruled over busy, prosperous communities. In northwest Africa, the kings of Mali were world famous for the fabulous treasure they owned, as well as for the fairness and justice of their rule. They gained their wealth from the rich goldfields in and around their lands.

TRADE Merchants from Europe and the Middle East made the long camel trek across the dry, empty Sahara Desert to bring back trade goods. They also made dangerous voyages along the west African coast to trade with these prosperous kingdoms, and to bring back gold and other treasure. They returned telling elaborate, exaggerated travelers' tales, full of unlikely incidents and improbable detail.

ISLAMIC INFLUENCE Many of these western kingdoms had been converted to Islam. Some of the impressive Islamic buildings–mosques, colleges and tombs–dating from this period still survive today, despite damage by centuries of harsh tropical weather. The city of Timbuktu in present-day Mali became a center of Islamic learning, attracting scholars from the wide expanse of Africa south of the Sahara.

GREAT ZIMBABWE In the southeastern part of the continent, there was another flourishing civilization, also based on gold, centered on the fortress-city of Great Zimbabwe. Elsewhere in eastern Africa, people mined iron ore and produced other valuable commodities, such as salt, leather, ivory and dried fish. They traded these goods with Arab merchants, who sailed along the east coast of Africa to the countries known today as Kenya, Tanzania and Mozambique.

There was also a profitable trade in slaves, who were employed as domestic servants throughout the Middle East. Today slavery is not tolerated, but it was widespread in many parts of the world (including southern Europe) during the Middle Ages.

EVIDENCE FOR THE AFRICAN LIFESTYLE There are few written sources describing the lives of many of the peoples living on the African continent during the Middle Ages. But archaeological evidence has revealed to us that they had developed a way of life that was remarkably well adapted to their surroundings. Sometimes they grew crops, sometimes they lived off traveling flocks and herds, depending on the soil and climatic conditions.

Surviving examples of African art also tell us that these peoples had a complex and sophisticated system of beliefs. This involved ancestral spirits, the forces of nature (such as wind and weather), sacred places, animals, trees or objects. This period also saw a number of major changes in the 'human landscape' of Africa, as various groups and peoples left their homelands and migrated toward new and more productive territory.

Kingdoms of Africa During the Middle Ages

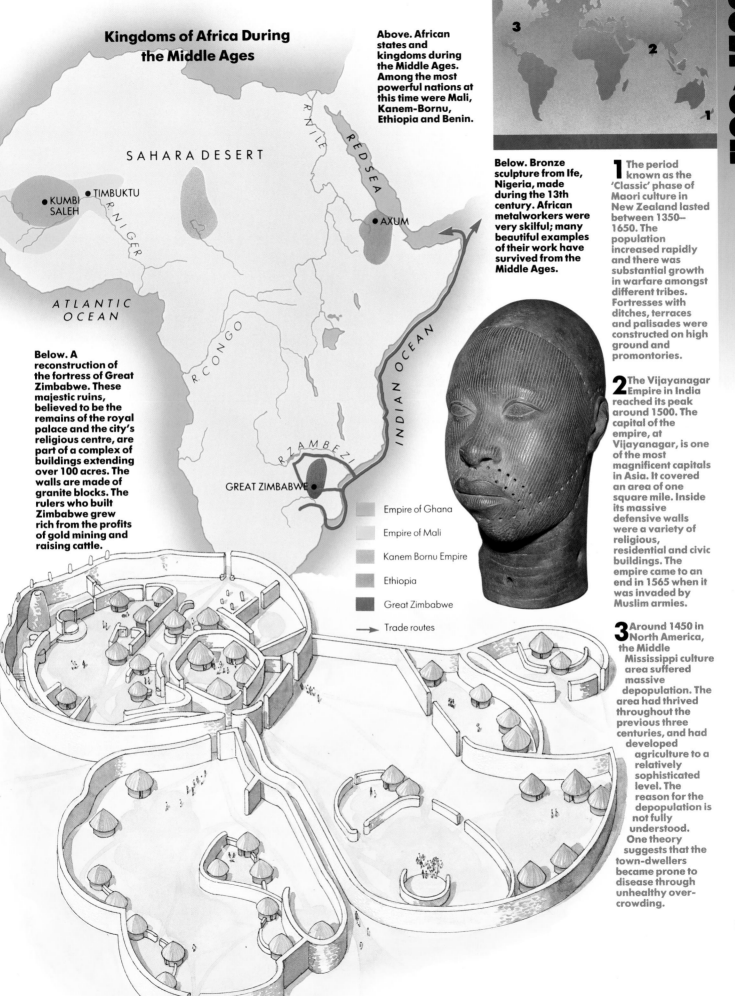

Above. African states and kingdoms during the Middle Ages. Among the most powerful nations at this time were Mali, Kanem-Bornu, Ethiopia and Benin.

Below. Bronze sculpture from Ife, Nigeria, made during the 13th century. African metalworkers were very skilful; many beautiful examples of their work have survived from the Middle Ages.

Below. A reconstruction of the fortress of Great Zimbabwe. These majestic ruins, believed to be the remains of the royal palace and the city's religious centre, are part of a complex of buildings extending over 100 acres. The walls are made of granite blocks. The rulers who built Zimbabwe grew rich from the profits of gold mining and raising cattle.

SAHARA DESERT

KUMBI SALEH

TIMBUKTU

R. NILE

RED SEA

AXUM

R. NIGER

ATLANTIC OCEAN

R. CONGO

INDIAN OCEAN

R. ZAMBEZI

GREAT ZIMBABWE

Empire of Ghana

Empire of Mali

Kanem Bornu Empire

Ethiopia

Great Zimbabwe

→ Trade routes

1 The period known as the 'Classic' phase of Maori culture in New Zealand lasted between 1350–1650. The population increased rapidly and there was substantial growth in warfare amongst different tribes. Fortresses with ditches, terraces and palisades were constructed on high ground and promontories.

2 The Vijayanagar Empire in India reached its peak around 1500. The capital of the empire, at Vijayanagar, is one of the most magnificent capitals in Asia. It covered an area of one square mile. Inside its massive defensive walls were a variety of religious, residential and civic buildings. The empire came to an end in 1565 when it was invaded by Muslim armies.

3 Around 1450 in North America, the Middle Mississippi culture area suffered massive depopulation. The area had thrived throughout the previous three centuries, and had developed agriculture to a relatively sophisticated level. The reason for the depopulation is not fully understood. One theory suggests that the town-dwellers became prone to disease through unhealthy over-crowding.

NORTH AMERICA AND THE CARIBBEAN

Totem poles from the village of Kispiox, British Columbia, in Canada. The carvings show magical creatures, and scenes from family history.

Several flourishing civilizations occupied the vast landmass of North America during the Middle Ages. Archaeologists have estimated that there were over 100 different languages spoken there round about 1500. All these different peoples did not live in isolation. Small groups joined together under the protection of a strong local leader, or were conquered and controlled by a powerful empire. Other 'families' of peoples were linked by a common ancestry, or by shared religious beliefs and traditions.

TRADE ROUTES Long-distance trade routes crossed the country, enabling goods and raw materials from one region to be exchanged for local produce from another. Trading contacts also helped new ideas and inventions in farming, warfare and craft techniques to spread over a wide area.

EVIDENCE OF THE AMERICAN PAST Few of these early Americans left any written records, but many of the objects they manufactured–buildings, *earthworks*, pottery, textiles, metalwork and jewelry–have

survived until today. In recent years, archaeologists have also used a number of scientific techniques to discover more about the early American people. Fragments of wood, the contents of rubbish pits, shriveled grains and seeds, ruined storehouses and burial mounds have revealed what people ate, what animals they farmed or hunted, what crops they grew and what clothes they wore.

The early European explorers regarded the native Americans as little more than savages, but the archaeological remains tell a different story. They reveal that early American societies were well organized, very skilled and often wealthy. They also show that the American peoples had developed a number of different ways of life, all designed to make the best use of the soils, climate and vegetation of the region in which they lived.

ANCIENT CITIES Among the most impressive remains dating from the Middle Ages in America are the great walled cities of the Chaco people, who lived in the southwest between 950–1300. The Mississippi people, who lived in the river valleys of the southeast, also built huge cities. During the 11th–13th centuries, their capital city, Cahokia, had about 10,000 inhabitants, and was larger than either London or Paris. Mississippi farmers developed an intensive system of cropping based on corn, beans and *squash*. These provided a well balanced vegetarian diet for the city population.

In the northeast, coastal peoples lived in wealthy village communities organized around fishing, hunting and trapping. They built strong wooden houses decorated with magnificent carvings. Further inland, in the great plains, villages were defended by deep moats, strong walls and stockades. Houses were large, and provided shelter and protection for several families living together. In each village, deep pits were dug to store grain for food during the cold winter months.

THE CARIBBEAN In the far south, the islands of the Caribbean were inhabited by the Arawak and Carib peoples. They were fishers and farmers, growing plentiful crops of tropical plants, especially *manioc* (for flour), pineapples, peanuts, beans and peppers. They wove cotton cloth, molded fine pottery and little clay statues, and were famous for their skill at making musical instruments.

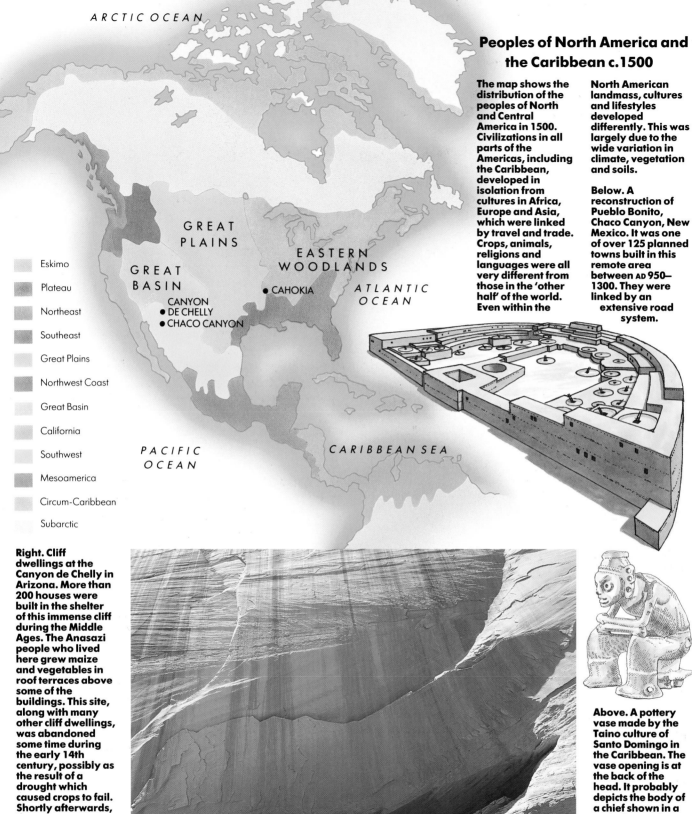

ARCTIC OCEAN

GREAT
PLAINS

GREAT
BASIN

EASTERN
WOODLANDS

• CAHOKIA

ATLANTIC
OCEAN

CANYON
• DE CHELLY
• CHACO CANYON

PACIFIC
OCEAN

CARIBBEAN SEA

■ Eskimo

■ Plateau

■ Northeast

■ Southeast

■ Great Plains

■ Northwest Coast

■ Great Basin

■ California

■ Southwest

■ Mesoamerica

■ Circum-Caribbean

■ Subarctic

Peoples of North America and the Caribbean c.1500

The map shows the distribution of the peoples of North and Central America in 1500. Civilizations in all parts of the Americas, including the Caribbean, developed in isolation from cultures in Africa, Europe and Asia, which were linked by travel and trade. Crops, animals, religions and languages were all very different from those in the 'other half' of the world. Even within the North American landmass, cultures and lifestyles developed differently. This was largely due to the wide variation in climate, vegetation and soils.

Below. A reconstruction of Pueblo Bonito, Chaco Canyon, New Mexico. It was one of over 125 planned towns built in this remote area between AD 950–1300. They were linked by an extensive road system.

Right. Cliff dwellings at the Canyon de Chelly in Arizona. More than 200 houses were built in the shelter of this immense cliff during the Middle Ages. The Anasazi people who lived here grew maize and vegetables in roof terraces above some of the buildings. This site, along with many other cliff dwellings, was abandoned some time during the early 14th century, possibly as the result of a drought which caused crops to fail. Shortly afterwards, the area was invaded by nomadic peoples, including the Apache. This brought the Anasazi settled, farming, lifestyle to an end.

Above. A pottery vase made by the Taino culture of Santo Domingo in the Caribbean. The vase opening is at the back of the head. It probably depicts the body of a chief shown in a typical seated burial position. Small pottery objects like this have been found in several sites throughout the Caribbean.

AZTECS AND INCAS

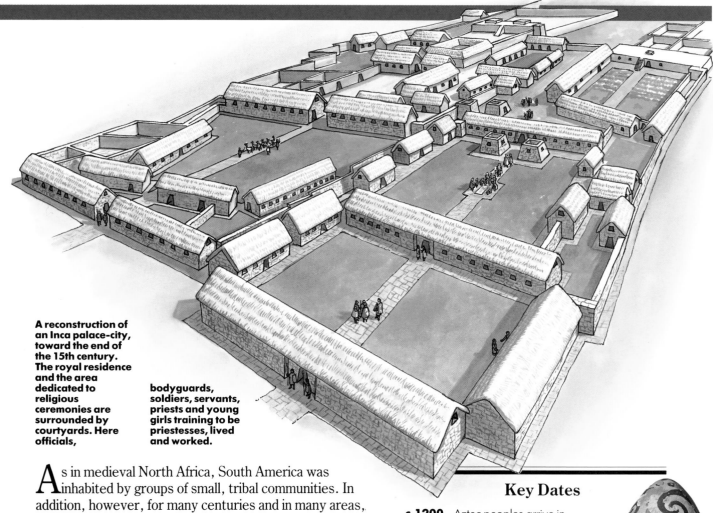

A reconstruction of an Inca palace-city, toward the end of the 15th century. The royal residence and the area dedicated to religious ceremonies are surrounded by courtyards. Here officials, bodyguards, soldiers, servants, priests and young girls training to be priestesses, lived and worked.

As in medieval North Africa, South America was inhabited by groups of small, tribal communities. In addition, however, for many centuries and in many areas, the tribal peoples had been brought under the control of powerful empires. Kings and priests living in great cities ruled over the surrounding lands, and demanded taxes or tribute from all the local inhabitants.

THE EMPIRES   In the later Middle Ages the two most powerful peoples in Central and South America were the Aztecs and the Incas. The Aztecs ruled over an empire based in present-day Mexico. The Incas controlled a long stretch of territory along the east coast, from present-day Bolivia to the far south of Peru. The Aztec and Inca Empires were rich, terrifying and very powerful. But they were both destroyed by the arrival of European soldiers during the first half of the sixteenth century.

The Aztecs seized power during the 14th century, replacing earlier Mexican civilizations–the Toltec, Zapotec and Mixtec–but continuing many of their traditions and beliefs. Aztec society was highly organized and strictly

Key Dates

c.1200	Aztec peoples arrive in Mexico from the north
1350–1475	Aztec Empire established
Pre–1400	Inca peoples established as one of many small groups living in Andes Mountains
1428	Aztecs take control of whole valley area of central Mexico
1476	Incas conquer powerful neighboring Chimu kingdom
1521	Cortes takes control of all Mexico. End of Aztec power
1533	Pizarro captures Inca capital city of Cuzco, and controls Peru, Bolivia and Ecuador. End of Inca power

Right. Pottery figure of an Inca warrior, from the northern part of the Inca Empire.

64

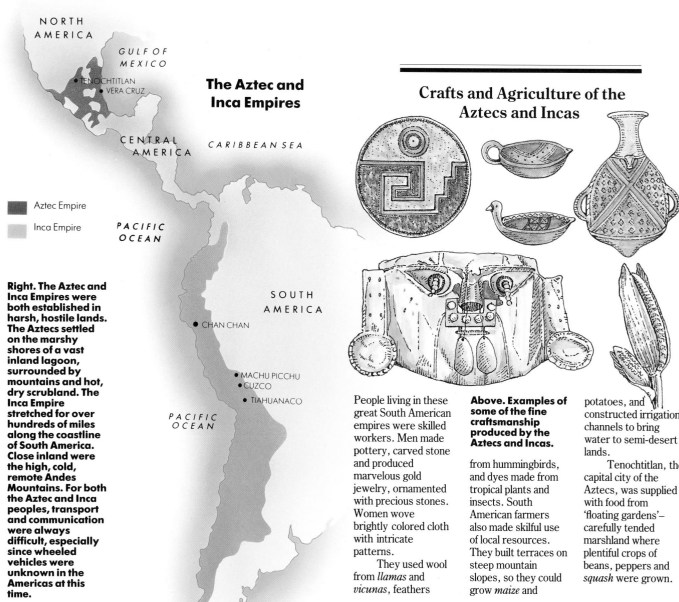

The Aztec and Inca Empires

Right. The Aztec and Inca Empires were both established in harsh, hostile lands. The Aztecs settled on the marshy shores of a vast inland lagoon, surrounded by mountains and hot, dry scrubland. The Inca Empire stretched for over hundreds of miles along the coastline of South America. Close inland were the high, cold, remote Andes Mountains. For both the Aztec and Inca peoples, transport and communication were always difficult, especially since wheeled vehicles were unknown in the Americas at this time.

Aztec Empire

Inca Empire

Crafts and Agriculture of the Aztecs and Incas

People living in these great South American empires were skilled workers. Men made pottery, carved stone and produced marvelous gold jewelry, ornamented with precious stones. Women wove brightly colored cloth with intricate patterns.

They used wool from *llamas* and *vicunas*, feathers

Above. Examples of some of the fine craftsmanship produced by the Aztecs and Incas.

from hummingbirds, and dyes made from tropical plants and insects. South American farmers also made skilful use of local resources. They built terraces on steep mountain slopes, so they could grow *maize* and

potatoes, and constructed irrigation channels to bring water to semi-desert lands.

Tenochtitlan, the capital city of the Aztecs, was supplied with food from 'floating gardens'–carefully tended marshland where plentiful crops of beans, peppers and *squash* were grown.

---

controlled. Trade, farming and craftworking flourished, and magnificent cities and monuments were built. But the emperor and his officials were feared and hated by many of the ordinary people whom the Aztecs conquered. Some historians have even suggested that the ordinary Aztec people welcomed the European soldiers who came in the 16th century as liberators, who would set them free.

AZTEC SOCIETY AND BELIEFS Like many South American societies, the Aztec civilization was based on war. Battles were necessary to provide a steady stream of captives to be killed as sacrifices to the gods. The Aztecs believed that if they stopped offering human blood and hearts to the gods, then the sun would stop shining, and crops and people would die.

INCA SOCIETY AND BELIEFS The Incas took control–though for less than one century–in Peru during the early 15th century. They conquered the neighboring Chimu Empire, which had ruled a large territory around its capital city of Chan-Chan in the north of the country.

Like the Aztecs, the Incas demanded complete obedience from the people they ruled. They also imposed heavy taxes. Inca tax-collectors took two-thirds of all crops grown, in return for providing food and shelter for anyone who became too sick or old to look after themselves. The state also started vast construction projects, such as the great city at Cuzco, which were enormously expensive, and employed hundreds of thousands of workers.

ROUTES OF COMMUNICATION Inca officials kept detailed records of taxes and other administrative matters on *qipus*–carefully knotted string. These qipus show that the Inca Empire was highly organized, with a large army and many government servants. There was also a network of government roads linking distant parts of the empire. Messengers hurried along with urgent orders, and armies marched with bands of protesting captives on their way to forced resettlement in regions far from their homes. Ordinary people were not allowed to travel on these roads without a special permit.

Medieval people were great travelers, even though journeys were slow, uncomfortable and exhausting.

MODES OF TRANSPORT Ordinary people plodded wearily on foot, or jogged and jolted along on horses and camels. Wealthy people could afford well upholstered carts, but these frequently got stuck or were overturned in the deep ruts and potholes which scarred the surfaces of many medieval roads. The most comfortable way to travel was probably by litter–an enclosed 'cabin' slung on poles between two or four horses–but this was usually reserved for royal ladies or clergymen.

DANGERS OF TRAVEL Medieval travelers faced danger, as well as discomfort, along the way. Attacks by highway robbers, pirates and bandits were common. Shipwrecks, landslides, floods, bitter cold and searing heat all caused loss of life. It was hardly surprising that people came to believe that particularly desolate stretches of countryside, like the Gobi Desert in China, were haunted by evil spirits, lying in wait to lure unwary travelers to a certain death.

REASONS FOR TRAVEL Why, then, did medieval people travel? First, to make money. We have already seen how merchants covered vast distances, by land and sea,

The Travels of Ibn Battuta

Ibn Battuta was born in North Africa around 1300. He trained as a lawyer, but spent most of his life in adventurous travel. We know about his exploits because he dictated his memoirs to a secretary in 1363, and copies of this book have survived. As you can see from the map, he traveled an extraordinary distance during his lifetime.

to bring valuable goods from China and India to markets in the Middle East and Europe.

Some medieval people traveled in search of food. For example, fishermen from northern Europe made the long and dangerous journey to the icy Arctic waters off Norway to bring back huge catches of cod. These were dried and salted for use in winter.

The dangers of travel by sea. A shipwreck, dramatically illustrated in a 14th century Italian manuscript.

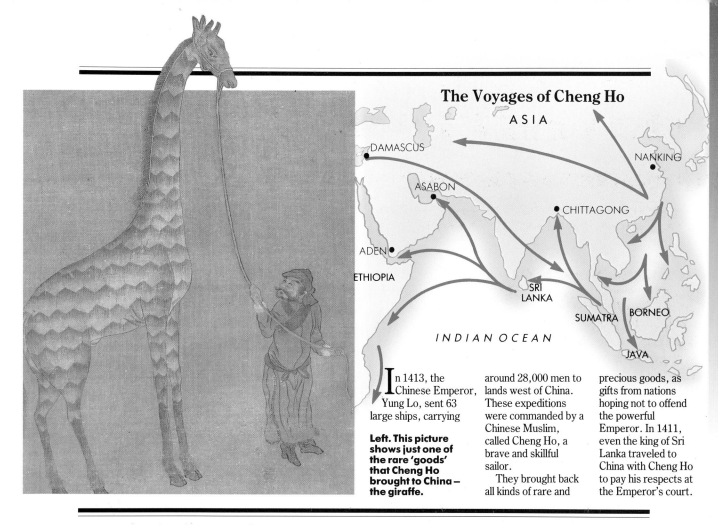

The Voyages of Cheng Ho

ASIA

DAMASCUS

NANKING

ASABON

CHITTAGONG

ADEN

ETHIOPIA

SRI LANKA

SUMATRA BORNEO

JAVA

INDIAN OCEAN

In 1413, the Chinese Emperor, Yung Lo, sent 63 large ships, carrying around 28,000 men to lands west of China. These expeditions were commanded by a Chinese Muslim, called Cheng Ho, a brave and skillful sailor.

They brought back all kinds of rare and precious goods, as gifts from nations hoping not to offend the powerful Emperor. In 1411, even the king of Sri Lanka traveled to China with Cheng Ho to pay his respects at the Emperor's court.

Left. This picture shows just one of the rare 'goods' that Cheng Ho brought to China – the giraffe.

The farming and fishing communities of Polynesia also traveled long distances. They sailed in fragile boats across the vast Pacific Ocean to found new settlements on fertile volcanic islands.

Religion was a third reason why people traveled during the Middle Ages. Believers from many different faiths went on *pilgrimages* to holy places all over the world. Muslims visited Mecca. Christians traveled to Jerusalem, Rome and the shrines of various saints throughout Europe. In India and the surroundings lands, Hindu and Buddhist pilgrims traveled to pray at temples, or to listen to holy men and religious teachers.

All these pilgrims, whatever their religion, saw their journeys as a time for thinking about God and the right way to live. In addition, for many people a pilgrimage was also a long, exciting and enjoyable vacation.

VOYAGES OF DISCOVERY Some medieval travelers needed no excuse for their journeys. Like people who go on vacation today, they simply wanted to see the world and to escape from everyday routine. In every country, villagers flocked to nearby towns to enjoy markets and fairs, or to take part in festivals. A few brave, daring, and, usually, wealthy invididuals made longer journeys, spurred on by curiosity and by the wish to discover all they could about distant lands.

We know about some of these travelers because

Left. An illustration from *Sir John Mandeville's Travels*. This was a popular (but largely fictitious) book describing several adventurous journeys. It was written in the 14th century, and translated into many European languages. This scene shows a mysterious group of philosophers, who, according to Mandeville's book, lived on the top of Mount Athos, in Greece.

records of their amazing journeys have survived. Marco Polo (who traveled through China), Ibn Fadlan (who journeyed overland from Baghdad to the Viking kingdoms of Russia and Scandinavia), Ibn Battuta (a Muslim from North Africa who spent 20 years traveling in Asia and India) and Cheng Ho (a Chinese explorer who made daring voyages through the South China Seas) all left descriptions of their adventures, full of fascinating details about the lands and peoples they visited.

SAILORS AND SCHOLARS

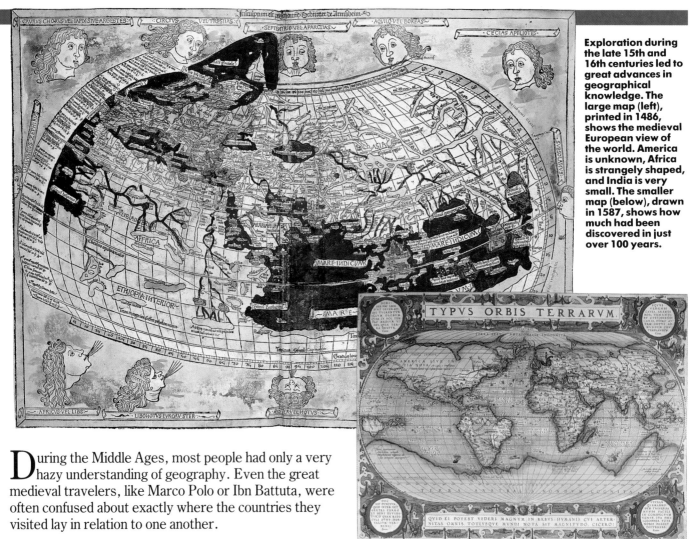

Exploration during the late 15th and 16th centuries led to great advances in geographical knowledge. The large map (left), printed in 1486, shows the medieval European view of the world. America is unknown, Africa is strangely shaped, and India is very small. The smaller map (below), drawn in 1587, shows how much had been discovered in just over 100 years.

During the Middle Ages, most people had only a very hazy understanding of geography. Even the great medieval travelers, like Marco Polo or Ibn Battuta, were often confused about exactly where the countries they visited lay in relation to one another.

GEOGRAPHICAL DISCOVERIES There were two groups of people in medieval times who did, however, know a great deal about the earth's surface. These were sailors and scholars. Geographers, mathematicians and astronomers made calculations and performed experiments to discover more accurate ways of measuring time and distance.

By the time Marco Polo set out on his travels in the late 13th century, leading scholars were convinced that the earth was round, and not flat, as earlier people had believed. But they still had no clear idea of the shape and size of the different continents, nor of how much of the globe was covered by dry land, and how much by the sea.

THE SCIENCE OF NAVIGATION Unlike the scholars, most sailors could not read and write, but they studied coastlines, tides, currents, winds and weather. By the 15th century, the knowledge of the scholars, and the sailors' practical skills began to be combined. European rulers, like Prince Henry 'the Navigator' of Portugal, encouraged travel and exploration. Prince Henry even set up a training college for would-be adventurers.

There was a financial reason for this government interest in travel, as well. Wars in Asia, and the capture of Constantinople (Istanbul) by Muslim troops in 1453, disrupted overland trade with the East. People began to wonder whether they could find a sea route to India which would mean that they did not have to rely on overland travel.

In the late 15th century Portuguese sailors set off to explore west Africa, and to see what lay beyond. This was, for them, a brave and risky venture. Some old-

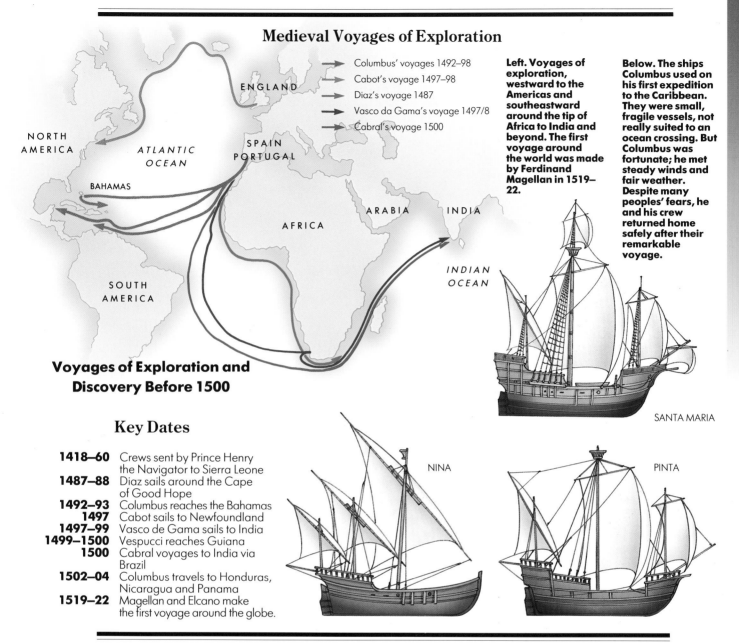

Medieval Voyages of Exploration

→ Columbus' voyages 1492–98
→ Cabot's voyage 1497–98
→ Diaz's voyage 1487
→ Vasco da Gama's voyage 1497/8
→ Cabral's voyage 1500

ENGLAND

NORTH AMERICA

ATLANTIC OCEAN

SPAIN
PORTUGAL

BAHAMAS

ARABIA INDIA

AFRICA

SOUTH AMERICA

INDIAN OCEAN

Left. Voyages of exploration, westward to the Americas and southeastward around the tip of Africa to India and beyond. The first voyage around the world was made by Ferdinand Magellan in 1519–22.

Below. The ships Columbus used on his first expedition to the Caribbean. They were small, fragile vessels, not really suited to an ocean crossing. But Columbus was fortunate; he met steady winds and fair weather. Despite many peoples' fears, he and his crew returned home safely after their remarkable voyage.

SANTA MARIA

NINA

PINTA

Voyages of Exploration and Discovery Before 1500

Key Dates

1418–60	Crews sent by Prince Henry the Navigator to Sierra Leone
1487–88	Diaz sails around the Cape of Good Hope
1492–93	Columbus reaches the Bahamas
1497	Cabot sails to Newfoundland
1497–99	Vasco de Gama sails to India
1499–1500	Vespucci reaches Guiana
1500	Cabral voyages to India via Brazil
1502–04	Columbus travels to Honduras, Nicaragua and Panama
1519–22	Magellan and Elcano make the first voyage around the globe.

fashioned scholars warned that they would be burned up in seas of fire, or swallowed by terrible monsters, if they traveled too far south.

JOURNEYS TO INDIA In 1498, a fleet led by Vasco da Gama landed triumphantly in western India, and returned home safely to Portugal. But the eastward route to India proved to be very long, and very costly.

A few sailors began to wonder whether they could reach the eastern lands by traveling westward. They had heard strange rumors about floating islands and mysterious shapes on the horizon. In the late 14th century, the Vivaldi brothers sailed westward, but vanished without trace. Perhaps the old geographers, like Ptolemey, were right, and the dry lands of the world were ringed by an endless ocean, where travelers could

drift forever, lost and without hope?

CHRISTOPHER COLUMBUS A young and inexperienced sailor, named Christopher Columbus, was determined to prove these theories wrong. He was certain he could reach India by traveling west, and that his journey would be quicker than the eastward route. Columbus spent many years trying to raise money to buy ships.

At last, in 1492, he set sail, and, after a smooth and easy voyage, he sighted land. Eagerly, he searched the shore for the fabulous riches of the East described by Marco Polo and other travelers to China. But all he found were fragile thatched huts, and timid, friendly people, dressed simply in cotton cloth ornamented with shells and feathers. Was this really the fabulous East?

THE NEW WORLD

When Columbus first sighted land, he recorded in his journal that he had arrived in Japan. For the rest of his life, Columbus maintained that he had reached the Far East, and never gave up hope of finding rich stores of gold and jewels.

Today we know that the land where he first came ashore was one of the Bahamas Islands, off the coast of Florida. Columbus may not have sailed to the Indies, but he had, by chance, arrived on the edge of a vast 'new' continent, which no one in Europe had imagined to exist.

AMERICA The explorers who came after him named this unknown land America, after Amerigo Vespucci, who traveled there in 1499. But to many Europeans, throughout the sixteenth and seventeenth centuries, it became, simply, the 'New World.' Of course, as we have seen on pages 62–65, this land was not 'new' at all. It was inhabited by a number of different peoples, who had developed skilled and well organized civilizations.

In addition, although they did not know it, Columbus and the other late-medieval explorers were not the first Europeans to travel there. Around the year 1000, Viking sailors had established settlements on the northeast coast, in present-day Canada. And recently discovered cave paintings in the Caribbean suggest that either the Vivaldi brothers (see page 68) did reach America, only to perish on the homeward voyage, or that West African peoples had also made the crossing from their homes on the other side of the Atlantic Ocean.

Stone jaguar, from a temple in the Maya-Toltec city of Chichen Itza. The Mayas and Toltecs were the most powerful peoples in Central America before the Aztecs came to power.

THE EUROPEAN INVASION OF AMERICA The years following Columbus' arrival in the Americas were unhappy ones. The Europeans, armed with powerful weapons, and able to travel swiftly on horseback, quickly overpowered the local peoples. They also exploited them in their search for gold, jewels and other exotic treasures. The Aztec and Inca leaders were hunted down and killed.

European weapons and, worse still, infectious diseases, such as measles and smallpox, soon wiped out a large number of native Americans. A few missionary priests had the courage to try and stop the heartless destruction of the 'New World' civilizations and their peoples. But the damage had been done. European governors were appointed, and the New World was turned into a profitable *colonial empire*, whose main purpose was to supply gold, silver and other valuable goods to the kings of Spain and Portugal.

THE INFLUENCE OF AMERICA Although cruelly exploited, the 'New World' and its people did have a powerful effect on the countries of Europe. Many new crops, which before grew only in America, were imported, and soon became part of everyday life. New ideas, words, and technologies were described in the reports brought back by travelers.

Most important of all, the maps had to be redrawn. Columbus and his discoveries had–for sailors and scholars throughout Europe–literally changed the world.

Metals from South America

The Spanish explorers and conquerors of South America greedily plundered their newly acquired lands. Many Aztec and Inca treasures were looted, and local peoples were cruelly made to work like slaves in the rich South American mines. The Spaniards brought back vast amounts of silver, gold and precious stones to Europe. Most of the silver was minted into coins. These imports of silver caused rapid price inflation in Europe, particularly Spain.

Inca statue (made of solid silver) of a man holding a set of pan pipes, a typical Andean instrument.

New Foods from the Americas

Above. European scholars, kings, princes and fortune hunters were all fascinated by travelers' descriptions of the landscape and peoples of America. Many expeditions set out to explore the territory, most spurred on by greed for treasure and gold. This map of South America was produced in France around 1550. It shows how much of the continent had become known to Europeans in a very short time.

Right. Gold mask, probably used to cover the face of a mummified corpse, from Colombia, South America. Severed heads and masks, sometimes in the form of skeleton faces, have been found at many sites in South America. They are mostly very finely made, using gold, silver and precious stones.

European travelers brought several new plants and animals back with them from the Americas. These unknown species aroused great interest and, sometimes, suspicion. For many years, they remained expensive luxuries,

All the above vegetables, fruits and animals were new to Europeans in the 16th century.

although eventually some, like the potato (11) and the tomato (3), became widely grown in many lands around the world.

Among the other important plants from America were red and black kidney beans (10), marrows and pumpkins (sometimes called squashes) (1), corn, sunflowers (2), cocoa beans (used to make chocolate) (6), red and green peppers (5), pineapples (12) and tobacco (4). Sweet potatoes (9) and cactus (7, 8), were introduced into southern Europe. In spite of their name, Turkeys (13) also came from the west, not from eastern lands.

Crisis and Change
TIME CHART

	EUROPE	MUSLIM WORLD	CHINA AND THE EAST	REST OF WORLD
1206		Mongol invasions westward begin		
1234			Mongols destroy Chin Empire	
1275			Marco Polo arrives in China; works for Kublai Khan	
1299		Ottoman Turks start to grow powerful; lead Muslim world toward recovery		
1315	Famines, caused by bad weather and perhaps overpopulation			
1337	Hundred Years War begins between England and France			
1341			Black Death epidemic starts in Asia	
1346		Black Death kills thousands in Middle East		
1347>9	Black Death kills about one-third of the total population			
1368			Ming Dynasty takes control of China from Mongols Vijayanagar Empire becomes powerful in south India	
1377		Death of Ibn Battuta, famous Muslim traveler and explorer		
1400				Malacca (in East Indies) established as great international trading center
1400>1550	Italian Renaissance; "rebirth" of culture			
1405			Chinese travelers explore westward	
1415				Portuguese capture Ceuta, north Africa; it becomes base for colonial expansion
1428	Joan of Arc leads French armies in Hundred Years War			
1430				Great stone palace-city built at Zimbabwe
1445	First book printed in Europe			
1458		Ottoman Turks capture Constantinople; end of Byzantine Empire		
1470				Inca Empire expands in Peru
1478	Ivan the Terrible, Czar (king) of Russia, finally expels Mongols from his lands			
1492				Columbus crosses the Atlantic
1497				British explorer John Cabot sails across North Atlantic to Newfoundland
1498			Vasco da Gama makes first voyage to India from Europe	
1519				Cortes begins conquest of Aztec Empire
1520>1566		Reign of Sultan Suleiman the Magnificent		
1532				Pizarro begins conquest of Inca Empire

acupuncture   A system of medicine, originating in China, which aims to treat illness or relieve pain by harmonizing the energy that flows along "meridians" (invisible channels in the body). Fine needles are inserted at key points in the system of meridians, to stimulate or unblock the energy flow.

amulets   Magic charms.

anthropology   The study of how people in different cultures and societies live and behave.

archaeology   The study of the past from physical remains— buildings, pottery, metalwork, fragments of cloth, etc.—and from the traces these objects have left behind them in the ground.

bacteria   Minute living organisms, too small to see with the naked eye. Some bacteria are beneficial to humans (for example, they can help digestion), but others cause dangerous diseases.

Black Death   An old name for bubonic plague, a deadly disease caused by the bacterium *pasturella pestis*. The Black Death killed millions of people in the medieval world.

Buddhism   A religious philosophy followed by many people in India and the Far East, during the medieval period and today. Buddhists follow the teachings and example of Siddhartha Gautama, called the Buddha, a gentle, learned philosopher who lived in the 5th century BC.

caliphs   Muslim rulers.

calligraphy   Beautiful writing. Medieval scribes wrote with pens made from feathers or (in eastern lands) from reeds and bamboo.

caravanserai   A lodging house for travelers (often merchants) and their pack-animals, found in central Asia and the Middle East.

Cardinal   One of the most important figures in the Catholic Church. The College of Cardinals elects the Pope and helped to decide on church policy.

Catalan Atlas   One of the earliest surviving books of maps based on accurate surveying and measurement, rather than on an imaginary picture of the world. It was made during the 14th century for King Charles V of France.

chivalry   The code of behavior that knights were meant to follow. A chivalrous knight was meant to be brave, bold, loyal, honorable, faithful, devout, charitable and loving.

city state   Self-governing community; in Italy, often comprised of a small, walled town and the surrounding fields.

colonial empire   A weaker or less "developed" territory ruled by a powerful country primarily for its own benefit, rather than for the good of its inhabitants.

Confucius   A Chinese philosopher who lived from about 551–478 BC. His teachings had a great influence on the development of Chinese civilization.

courtiers   Noble men and women who spent their lives as companions, advisers or helpers to kings, queens and other powerful people.

dhow   A light sailing ship, designed to carry goods across the Indian Ocean and the Arabian Sea.

dissection   Cutting up dead bodies, of people or animals, to discover more about how they worked and to improve the treatment of disease.

dynasty   Ruling family, where power is passed on from generation to generation.

earthworks   Solid mounds or walls made of earth, often used as military defenses.

feudal system   A way of organizing society, stretching from one powerful, wealthy person down to those with no power at all, in which land is granted in return for military or labor services.

garrison   Building where whole regiments of soldiers are lodged.

Gothic architecture   A graceful, elegant style of building and design which developed in northern Europe between the 12th and 15th centuries.

hierarchy   An ordered structure of control or command.

Hinduism   A religious philosophy followed by millions of people in India and the surrounding lands during the Middle Ages and today.

indulgences   Documents offering people pardon for all their sins, sold by the medieval church in return for a money payment, usually to a charitable cause. The system of indulgences—which had originated simply to encourage people to give money to good causes—was widely abused during the Middle Ages, and was fiercely criticized by religious thinkers of the Reformation.

Janissaries   Well-trained soldiers, originally from Christian families, who fought in the army of the Muslim Ottoman sultans, based in Constantinople.

junk   A Chinese sailing ship, designed to carry heavy loads of cargo across the South China Sea.

knights   Soldiers mounted on horseback; usually protected by chain-mail or plate armor and well equipped with weapons. Only rich men could afford a horse and all the fighting equipment, and so, before long, "knight" came to mean someone from a wealthy, high-status family and it was used as a honorable title, rather than as a military term.

llamas   Large animals, related to camels, found only in South America.

Magyars Nomadic people who lived and herded wild horses on the plains of eastern Europe.

maize A tall cereal crop, also known as "corn" or "sweetcorn."

manioc A tropical root crop, originating in the Americas.

Mongols The nomadic peoples who roamed the plains of central and northeastern Asia. They lived by rearing herds of horses and became excellent mounted warriors.

mosque A place where Muslims meet for prayer, to listen to sermons and to read the *Qur'an*.

mystic Someone who seeks to communicate with God through prayer and meditation, and who perhaps also receives "visions" or other experiences of God.

nomad Someone who does not live in a fixed, settled home, but who moves from place to place, in order to find food or water.

nosegay Bunch of sweet-smelling flowers, carried to disguise unpleasant smells. In the past, people believed that nosegays would also help to ward off disease.

pagan A word used by followers of a religious philosophy to describe people who do not share their beliefs. In medieval Europe, "pagan" meant anyone who was not a Christian.

penitents People who are sorry for their past sins and who say special prayers, or perform special rituals, to ask God for forgiveness.

physical remains The objects—documents, works of art, buildings, tombs, textiles, pottery, metalwork and, sometimes, even the whole landscape—created by past civilizations, which are studied by historians and archaeologists to discover information about the past.

pilgrimage A journey to a holy place, made by people from many religious traditions as a mark of their faith and devotion.

plague See **Black Death**, above.

prophet A messenger from God. People in many centuries and from many faiths have been regarded as prophets.

quipu A knotted sting, used by the Inca people of Central America to keep accounts and other records of business and military affairs.

quadrivium Part of the curriculum taught in medieval European schools and universities. It covered the following subjects: mathematics, music and astronomy.

Qur'an The holy book containing the message which, Muslims believe, God gave to the prophet Muhammad, to tell people how they ought to live.

Reformation A movement, originating in Europe during the late 15th century, which criticized the practices and the personnel of the Catholic Church, and made demands for reform.

relics Objects (sometimes parts of the body) thought to have belonged to saints or other holy people within the Christian tradition.

Renaissance A word meaning "re-birth," used to describe a movement in the arts, literature, music and philosophy, which flourished in late-medieval Europe.

samurai A Japanese warrior. Like knights, and for the same reasons, samurai came from the upper ranks of Japanese society. And, like knights, they too were meant to follow a strict code of brave, honorable behavior.

scribe A professional writer, employed to write letters, keep accounts and make copies of books. A scribe might also keep a record of events.

squash Plants related to melons, gourds and cucumbers, sometimes known as pumpkins.

steppes High, bleak, windswept plains, with low rainfall. Usually the only food plants which can survive there are grasses of various kinds.

sultan "Prince"; a word used to describe Muslim rulers.

totem pole A tall, beautifully decorated wooden pole, carved with scenes and faces recording the history of a family group. Totem poles were produced by American Indians living along the northwest Pacific coast, in present-day Canada.

trivium Part of the curriculum taught in medieval schools and universities. It covered the following subjects: grammar, linguistics and philosophy.

verjus The juice of unripe grapes, used as a seasoning (rather like lemon juice or vinegar today) and as a preservative.

vicunas South American animals closely related to the llama.

wood-block printing An early form of printing.

Zen Japanese Buddhist movement which developed in the 13th century. Zen aims at harmony in living and uses everyday arts, such as tea-making and calligraphy, to develop effortless skills.

INDEX

Further Reading

GENERAL REFERENCE
The Times Atlas of World History ed. by Geoffrey Barraclough (Hammond, 1989)
Arms and Armor by Michele Byam (Knopf, 1988)
The Middle Ages by Catherine Oakes (Harcourt Brace Jovanovich, 1989)
The Middle Ages: History of Everyday Things by Giovanni Caselli (Bedrick, Peter, 1988)
The Renaissance and the New World: History of Everyday Things by Giovanni Caselli (Bedrick, Peter, 1986)
The Middle Ages: Cultural Atlas for Young People by Mike Corbishley (Facts On File, 1990)

EUROPE
The Oxford Illustrated History of Medieval Europe ed. by George Holmes, (Oxford, 1990)

Medieval People by Sarah
Howarth (Millbrook, 1992)
Medieval Places by Sarah
Howarth (Millbrook, 1992)
*A Medieval Castle: Inside
Story* by Fiona MacDonald
(Bedrick, Peter, 1990)
*A Medieval Cathedral: Inside
Story* by Fiona MacDonald
(Bedrick, Peter, 1991)

THE REST OF THE WORLD

*Cultural Atlas of Ancient
America* by Michael Coe
(Facts On File, 1986)
Cultural Atlas of China by
Caroline Blunden (Facts
On File, 1983)
Cultural Atlas of Africa by
Jocelyn Murray (Facts On
File, 1981)
Islam by Abdul Latif Al Hood
(Watts, Franklin, 1907)

Picture Acknowledgments

The author and publishers would like to acknowledge, with thanks,
the following photographic sources:
Front cover (left and right) Werner Forman Archive; p. 10 C.M. Dixon; p. 11 Ancient Art &
Architecture Collection; p. 12 Barbara Heller Photo Library; p. 13 (left) Ancient Art &
Architecture Collection, (right) C.M. Dixon; p. 15 Ancient Art & Architecture Collection;
p. 17 (upper left) Sonia Halliday Photographs, (upper right) Werner Forman Archive, (lower)
C.M. Dixon; p. 19 (left) SCALA, (right) C.M. Dixon; p. 20 (left) AKG, (right) Ancient Art &
Architecture Collection; p. 21 (all photos) Stanley E. West; p. 22 AKG; p. 25 (upper and lower)
Ancient Art & Architecture Collection; p. 26 (upper) Werner Forman Archive, (center) C.M.
Dixon; p. 27 AKG; p. 28 SCALA; p. 29 Sonia Halliday Photographs; p. 31 Sonia Halliday
Photographs; p. 32 SCALA; p. 34 (upper and lower left) Ancient Art & Architecture Collection,
(center) Werner Forman Archive; p. 36 Werner Forman Archive; p. 37 Werner Forman
Archive; p. 38 (upper) Michael Holford, (lower) Ancient Art & Architecture Collection;
p. 39 (upper left) The British Library, (upper right) Ashmolean Museum, Oxford, (lower)
Michael Holford; p. 42 (upper) Robert Harding Picture Library, (lower) Sonia Halliday
Photographs; p. 44 Sonia Halliday Photographs; p. 45 Sonia Halliday Photographs; p. 46 (upper)
Robert Harding Picture Library, (lower) C.M. Dixon; p. 47 (upper left and right) C.M. Dixon,
(lower) Michael Holford; p. 48 (upper) C.M. Dixon, (lower) Ancient Art & Architecture
Collection; p. 50 Ancient Art & Architecture Collection; p. 51 The Chester Beatty Library;
p. 52 (upper) Ancient Art & Architecture Collection, (lower) Réunion des Musées National;
p. 53 Sonia Halliday Photographs; p. 54 C.M. Dixon; p. 55 (upper) Robert Harding Picture
Library, (middle) Österreichische Nationalbibliothek, Vienna, (lower) William MacQuitty;
p. 56 Michael Holford; p. 57 Robert Harding Picture Library; p. 58 William MacQuitty;
p. 59 (upper and lower) Ancient Art & Architecture Collection; p. 61 (upper) Ancient Art &
Architecture Collection, (lower) Robert Harding Picture Library; p. 63 Werner Forman Archive;
p. 64 Ancient Art & Architecture Collection; pp. 66 and 67 Trustees of the British Museum;
p. 69 Werner Forman Archive; p. 70 Michael Holford; p. 71 Werner Forman Archive.